ERICA - PART FOUR

Death, Hell and Heaven

Erica Mukisa Kimani and Timsimon Kimani

Life Is Spiritual Ministries

The "ERICA" series is a registered trademark - ERICA™

Unless otherwise indicated, all Scriptures marked are taken from the KING JAMES VERSION, public domain.
Scripture taken from the Amplified Bible, Copyright © 1954, 1958, 1962, 1964, 1965, 1987 by The Lockman Foundation. Used by permission.

Printed in the United States of America.

ISBN: 9798647100290

Editor: Pamela Brinkley
www.thepaperpulpit.com

Other publications by this author Erica Mukisa are:
Eighteen Years With Lucifer - Part Two
Witchcraft and Spiritual Warfare - Part Three
The Truth About Money (Timsimon Kimani)
(Other publications forthcoming)

Published by Erica Mukisa and Timsimon Kimani
P.O. Box 1929 - 00232
Ruiru, Kenya, East Africa

Table of Contents

Chapter Eleven - The Seventh Heaven

His Name Is Holy
All Creation Bows Before Him
David Plays The Harp
The Twenty Four Elders
The Women of God

Chapter Twelve - The Four Faces of God

The Face of a Man
The Face of a Lion
The Face of an Eagle
The Face of an Ox

Chapter Thirteen - The Throne of God

The Seven Spirits of God
The Trumpet Sounds
Dancing and Singing

Chapter Fourteen - GOD

Oh Father!

Chapter Fifteen - My Conversation With God

My Questions To The Almighty
He Speaks!
His Holy Hill

Chapter Sixteen - Leaving Heaven

God Answers My Mother's Prayer
Your Heavenly Investment
Blessed Koinonia

INTRODUCTION

My name is Erica Mukisa Kimani, I was born in 1991 on the 26th of August. I am the daughter of Emmanuel and Bernadette Waiswa, they are Sunday school teachers. I have one brother, Evans Mwesigwa. He is a minister of the gospel and as of 2nd of April 2020 he is studying theology in bible college. I started ministry on the 22nd of February 2009 as soon as I was delivered. Through my ministry I've seen thousands upon thousands coming to Christ and thousands getting delivered. I am a bachelors degree holder in Development Studies from Kampala International University, Uganda. I cannot count the number of churches I have visited preaching the gospel in Uganda. I have been to all of the districts in Uganda preaching the gospel. I have ministered at the border of Congo and Tanzania, Burundi, Rwanda, Kenya and Nigeria. My desire, since I started serving the Lord, has always been to win souls for Christ. It was through ministry that I met my husband Timsimon "Bamboo" Kimani. We met by divine appointment through Tommy Lee Osborn Owiti the son of the late Archbishop Silas Owiti and the current archbishop of Voice of Salvation and Healing Church in Kisumu, Kenya. Archbishop Silas Owiti was great friends with the late T.L. and Daisy Osborn of blessed memory. Tim and I met in 2017 during missionary work and we were married in 2019. We have faced many battles together including many attacks of witchcraft and sorcery. The attacks and battles we have fought are so numerous that we will write about them in forthcoming "Erica" publications. Tim has been very instrumental in helping me write all of my books and is also an author of the financial publication the "Truth About Money" a book which exposes the Satanic global banking system which dominates this world. Through every vicious attack of the devil, God has faithfully brought us through. His word is true:

> *"Many are the afflictions of the righteous: but the LORD delivereth him out of them all."*
>
> *(Psalms 34:19)*

This book is our fourth publication from the "ERICA" series. There are three other books which detail aspects of my testimony:

Erica Part One Seven Years In Hell
Erica Part Two Eighteen Years With Lucifer
Erica Part Three Witchcraft & Spiritual Warfare

These publications are great tools for the preaching of the gospel. Use them to help spread the gospel of the Kingdom of God.

> *"And if it seem evil unto you to serve the Lord, choose you this day whom ye will serve; whether the gods which your fathers served that were on the other side of the flood, or the gods of the Amorites, in whose land ye dwell: but as for me and my house, we will serve the Lord." (Joshua 24:15)*

CHAPTER ONE - THE ANGEL OF DEATH

My Initiation And Covenant With Death

When I was just eight years old my grandmother, A. Teosdoniah Ghandi took me to a graveyard where she initiated and covenanted me to the dead. Her own mother whom she sacrificed was also buried there. During this initiation, my grandmother performed rituals and named the lineage of my ancestors as she moved from grave to grave. There were about fourteen graves. She was sprinkling herbs on each grave and introducing me to each of the dead members of the family. As she continued, we finally got to the extreme end of the graveyard where her mother was buried. She sprinkled herbs on her grave as she held my hand and knelt down at the end of the grave. Then she sprinkled some water which was mixed with herbs on me. As she did so I was frozen and I could not move. I could feel the goosebumps on my skin and my hair was standing straight up and something was possessing me. My legs were shaking but I was standing straight up. It felt like the ground was about to open up and swallow me alive.

My Grandmother then laid herself down on her mother's grave and began to name her lineage and introduce me to the ancestors of the family. I then began to hear the voices coming from each grave one at a time, screaming (waaaaaaaaaaah!) and each grave had become an open portal for travel from this dimension to another dimension. I heard the voice of grandmother's mother asking angrily why she had exposed me to them at such a tender age. Grandmother replied that I was her heir and that a certain prophet had come into town from the United States and prophesied over my life saying that I would win many souls into the Kingdom of God. They would therefore have lost me if she did not initiate me immediately. Grandmother laid me down at the mouth of her mother's grave and I saw the shadow of death overshadowing me as a thick but thin dark smoke which entered into my nostrils and I became unconscious to the physical world around me. As soon as I became unconscious, a violent whirlwind snatched me out of my body and I found myself in the world of the dead. I was at the foot of hell! Hell is structured in the form of a human body. At the foot of hell, I was able to meet with my ancestors and the angel of death.

The Angel Of Death

The angel of death was traveling on a pale white horse. This horse has wings, it can fly and transform into a whirlwind. The discussion I had with my ancestors is in Erica Part One - Seven Years In Hell. For now I will proceed with what the angel of death showed me. The angel of death revealed to me the birds that he uses to transfer death through witchcraft. A crow, an owl, a bat, and a pigeon. The death angel took me to the valley of death and he told me that the reason why he keeps going there is because there is music that appeases his spirit and that music is of people who were murdered in cold blood and those who died prematurely like miscarriages, sacrifices, accidents, wars, sicknesses, suicides, abortions etc. The death angel told me that he whispers a song of death into people's ears and they commit suicide. He said he also whispered the same song into Judas Iscariot's ears after he had betrayed Jesus and he committed suicide. He said he is sustained by the death of humanity and he began to fly in the midst of the valley of death and as he began to fly I saw rivers of blood and he descended into the midst of the blood river and he was drinking it and swimming in it and he was covered in blood. He emerged out of the river at the end of it. The horse which he was riding on began to lick the blood which the death angel was covered with.

The Music Of The Dead

When he emerged from the blood river he looked young and attractive like Michael Jackson. The only difference between him and Michael was that he was more pale than Michael was. Death angel's lips were very red with blood. He was dressed just like Michael Jackson would dress in a black suit and top hat. Death angel told me that Michael Jackson and many other musicians and celebrities had traveled there for power and fame and he had given it (fame) to them. He said that they had entered into a covenant with him and in his music, the spirit of death would be transferred into the lives of the listeners. All of the breakdancing moves which they would do came from the angel of death. The celebrities would call him the "man in the mirror" or "rain man" or "boogie man," etc. Rihanna sang about the angel of death in a song entitled "Umbrella."

While the angel of death was transporting me into the world of the dead, I was traveling in a whirlwind and we were listening to Michael Jackson's song "thriller." The angel of death is *very* musical. Michael Jackson used to copy his moves and his looks. The "king of pop" was actually the angel of death. The angel of death was being ushered into this physical dimension through Michael Jackson. The angel of death showed me many musicians who had sold their souls to him. Westlife, Rihanna, Beyoncé, Jay-Z, Tupac Shakur, Selina, Celine Dione, Chris Brown, Puff Daddy, Shaggy, Snoop Doggy Dogg, Dr. Dre, Eminem, Brick & Lace, Shakira, Bob Marley, the list goes on and on. The angel of death assigned me to bring music into his kingdom and the music he was referring to was death through accidents. He explained to me that human beings are three-fold or tri-part. He said the life force of a human comes from the spirit or the heart of that human being.

So because of the life force or energy that comes from the spirit, man is able to do whatever he has set his heart on. The death angel told me that the key to accomplishing anything in the world was through meditation and concentration. So in order to cause accidents, I would need to concentrate and meditate and the more I did so, the more powerful I would become.

The angel of death told me that before Michael Jackson would record any song, he would go to a certain altar room in his house and lock himself in there for three days and astral project out of his body and travel into the world of the dead. The angel of death would sodomize him and impart a song and a skill into him before traveling back into his body. Then Michael would write exactly what he heard the angel of death singing and then go to the studio and record it. Before releasing the song, he would have to impart the spirits inside of him by molesting other young boys. Once that was done, he would take the master copies for rituals in order to have the songs enchanted with demonic energy. No music would be released without human sacrifice. Many people would die at Michael Jackson concerts because of the corrupted anointing which he would carry. Michael Jackson was Usher Raymond's god-father. Michael sodomized Usher in order to initiate him into the order. Usher Raymond was covenanted by the marine spirits in order to distribute spirits of immorality into his fan base. So when he would sing songs like "I wanna make love in this club," he would be ushering marine spirits from the marine kingdom into the physical dimension to enter into concert goers and fans. These fans would be sexually molested by these marine spirits and their lives would take on an immoral path. Marine spirits would covenant themselves with these unsuspecting fans and take over their lives. Because Usher Raymond carries a spirit of immorality, women will lust after him and throw their panties at him as he performs. His songs are homosexual anthems. Usher Raymond introduced Justin Bieber to the world and initiated him into the music industry. The entire music industry is covenanted together to Satan and to the angel of death. If they offer someone a deal, it is after one has been covenanted through a sex covenant. This sex covenant is usually a homosexual covenant performed and recorded on video. This is how the entire music and entertainment industry becomes one body. Hell is one body. Most entertainers will travel into the spirit world and receive "approval" from the kingdom of darkness before performing any role. These entertainers will have enhanced performance ability as a result of the "spirit" which behaviors them while they perform. This is what they call "getting into character." Through the spirit of a "muse" one can enhance their performance to a level of overwhelming ability resulting in worldly success and more open doors for more worldly success. However, this "success" comes at a price.

"For what shall it profit a man, if he shall gain the whole world, and lose his own soul?" Jesus Christ - (Mark 8:36)

The Scroll Of Corruption

The death angel unrolled a document the way one would unroll a scroll. In that scroll were the names of companies which work and belong to the angel of death. These companies become wealthy at the expense of the souls of men and the lives of people are taken in order to enrich these companies. The companies which manufacture cars, food, basically anything you can think of were tied in with him. Big media companies and global organizations are in covenant with him. I saw the names of the kings and queens of this world, the presidents and heads of state that are assigned under the angel of death were listed. Businessmen and captains of industry.

Traveling In A Whirlwind

After the angel of death revealed his secrets to me, he showed me how to come out of my body at will and travel into the spirit world and come back to my body. He also showed me how to travel in a whirlwind from one location to another. A sorcerer has the ability to travel from one place to another in a whirlwind with the help of the angel of death. The death angel showed me that man's body is dust and it can be transported from one point to another with the help of a whirlwind.

> *"When your fear cometh as desolation, and your destruction cometh as a whirlwind; when distress and anguish cometh upon you." (Proverbs 1:27)*

The whirlwind is a common mode of transportation in the realm of the spirit. The angel of death gave me a ring. He formed it from dust particles which became metallic and formed into a ring. Then he told me that because I was underage it would be invisible to others but visible to me. He instructed me that if I wanted to travel in the realm of the spirit, I only needed to think of the means by which I would travel and then I would touch the ring with my thumb even though I only had one ring on my left hand ring finger. I would make the same gesture on the other hand for reinforcement of concentration. With this same ring I could cause riots and conflicts among people and they would fight each other and shed blood. So from eight years of age I began working with the angel of death. After the initiation I went back into my body. I worked with the angel of death until I was eleven years old when I was taken by a very popular celebrity musician to meet with Satan face to face. The details of how I met with Satan are in my second book "Erica Part Two Eighteen Years With Lucifer."

CHAPTER TWO - HELL'S LAYOUT

While I served Satan, I learned that Hell is shaped in the structure of a human body. Hell is shaped as a man who is standing straight up but with the face of a serpent. The foot of hell is where you will find the gates of Hell, it's prisoners and prisons.

The Right Leg

The right leg of Hell keeps the souls of those who have died in sin. They are tortured and tormented in this place by demons in ways that are beyond the imagination. Their torment will never end. They are burnt, bruised, crushed, beaten, sexually abused and scratched by evil spirits. These lost souls long for death but death has been taken far from them. It is while they are there that they realize that even death sometimes can be a gift.

> *"And in those days shall men seek death, and shall not find it; and shall desire to die, and death shall flee from them." (Revelation 9:6)*

The Left Leg

The left leg of Hell imprisons those souls who are still physically alive. They are kept in different kinds of prisons depending on how they got there. Some arrived there through witchcraft. They were either personally involved in witchcraft or somebody bewitched them. Those who were involved in witchcraft were kept in coffins. Those who were bewitched were kept in chains of bondage. Others had their souls encaged in glass prisons. Others would just walk in and out of Hell at will. These were people who have special privileges In Hell due to their positions. These may be world leaders, witches, wizards, warlocks or low level servants of the devil who may be serving the devil but never even realize who they are serving. From the foot of hell one can see the head of Hell from a distance.

The Head Of Hell

The head of Hell is an altar that is built in the shape of a serpent with a pyramid in its mouth. The pyramid is inside the mouth of the serpent whose two fangs are above the eye on either side. On top of the pyramid sits the throne of Lucifer. The mouth of Hell is wide open. The pyramid is in the mouth of Hell. The throne of Satan is on top of the pyramid. The tongue of the serpent which represents deception is what runs the government of the kingdom of darkness and it stretches from beneath the throne of Satan which is above the pyramid, all the way down between the feet of hell.

The Eye Of Hell

In the eye of hell which is between the two fangs is another world which is filled with fashion and technology. This is where the fallen angels are. This is where I met with Cleo and other fallen angels like Abaddon (Apollyon of Revelation 9:11) and many other fallen angels. Cleo is in charge of all of the technology we see in this world. In the eye of Hell I saw laboratories where body parts of human beings were being mixed with technology in a way that allows humanity to merge with technology. This is the headquarters of artificial intelligence research. It is created here before it is exported into the world as new and cutting edge technological innovation. Facebook, whatsapp, Twitter, Instagram, IPhones, Computers, flatscreen TVs and telecom networks are all tools for Satan to spy on humanity and gather information. Cleo is the inventor of all of these new technologies. The printing of money and the creation of weapons of mass destruction, and every high tech vehicle like "the beast" which the United States President rides in are all creations of Cleo.

The high level sorcerers in Hollywood are well aware of whom and what they represent. They may veil the truth in satire, but they serve their father, the devil.

(fair use - for educational purposes)

(fair use - for educational purposes)

In the eye of Hell is where I saw the flags and logos of different countries, companies and organizations which we have here in the physical world. These companies disguise themselves as peacekeepers, food security organizations, health organizations etc. These companies manufacture everything human beings consume. It is in the eye of Hell that I saw the marine kingdom. I saw Jezebel, the Queen of the air, the Queen of the sea and the Queen of the coast. I saw Fortune 500 companies, international Stock Exchanges like NYSE and big media houses that are very well known here in the world. The big banks of the world, major universities, international schools and hospitals were all there.

The Heart Of Hell

In the heart of hell is where the lake of fire is. The lake of fire is in stages. It has a life of it's own and grows and produces terrible sounds. It is unending. It is a world of its own. There are beings that live in that fire and grow inside of it and flourish in the flames. They are in the shapes of caterpillars and maggots and spiders and roaches. They are huge in size. One cockroach can consume two people in a moment of time. I elaborate further about the lake of fire in "Erica Part One Seven Years In Hell".

"And death and hell were cast into the lake of fire. This is the second death." (Revelation 20:14)

"And the devil that deceived them was cast into the lake of fire and brimstone, where the beast and the false prophet are, and shall be tormented day and night for ever and ever." (Revelation 12:10)

The Right Hand

In the right hand of Hell is where the rulers of this world are located. These are the bloodlines of Satan who print the currency and control it's circulation. They run the financial system of the world. They influence politics and control the news. In other words, the controllers of this world are in the right hand of Hell. They are the synagogue of Satan. They include but are not limited to, the Pope, European royalty, the thirteen satanic bloodlines as explained in "The Truth About Money" by Timsimon Kimani.

The Left Hand

The left hand of Hell is where you find the puppets who appear to be leaders but are actually just the slaves of Satan. These are celebrities, politicians, news anchors, comedians, actors, entertainers, false prophets, sports stars, businessmen and captains of industry.

The Belly Of Hell

The belly of Hell is where you will find demons and evil spirits. Demons are the slaves and servants of the fallen angels. The belly of Hell is a bottomless pit and a wilderness. Even the demons hate that place because there is no life there. It is a place of emptiness. This is why demons will feed on a person if they get a chance.

They have no other source of nourishment. In Matthew 8:29 the demons screamed at Jesus:

> *"And, behold, they cried out, saying, What have we to do with thee, Jesus, thou Son of God? art thou come hither to torment us before the time?"*

The torment which demons dread is in the belly of Hell or in the right foot where, if they are sent, they are also tormented for failing in their missions. Even demons are tormented by superior demons for failing in their duties. The ancient Egyptian Pharaohs were replicas and manifestations of the priesthood of Hell. The children of Israel became slaves of Hell because they turned their backs on Heaven. They learned the ways of the Egyptians and forgot the ways of Yahweh. The result was devastating. The children of Israel became vain, they became witches and wizards, idolaters who, without the backing of Elohim, were as good as dead.

CHAPTER THREE - MY FIRST DEATH

At the age of sixteen I had my first encounter with death by actually dying. It happened after I had failed on a mission against a certain witch doctor who received the Lord Jesus Christ. His name was Musana. This was the same Musana I wrote about in Erica Part Three Witchcraft & Spiritual Warfare. After failing my mission to kill Musana for converting to Christianity, my soul was tortured and the pain would reflect in my body. I was rushed to the hospital because I had fainted. I felt pain in every part of my body but especially my head because Satan was bashing my head against the wall. When I was taken to the hospital the doctors tried every test they could but everything came back negative, but the pain was so severe they began treating me based on guess work. They prescribed powerful painkillers for me but the pain only got worse. The more I took pain killers the more the pain increased. I screamed so loud that the entire floor could hear me screaming out in pain. The doctors tried to inject me in order to put me to sleep but after injecting me I would fall weak and then begin screaming again. All of the doctors became interested in my case and they began to surround me and discuss what should be done in my case. One of the doctors pulled my mother aside and told her that my case was spiritual and that I should go to a powerful church or a powerful shrine for prayers or supernatural remedies.

The Doctors Give Up!

The doctors told my mother that they have done everything they can do for me. One doctor put a thermometer in my armpit. My temperature was high while my feet were freezing. The doctor asked if I had eaten, my mother replied that I only eat eggs. I would only eat eggs because of the snake system that had been covenanted to me as I described in Erica Part One Seven Years In Hell. The doctor was concerned and suggested that they should pour water on my head. So my mother held me up while my brother poured cold water on my head. Surprisingly, steam came from my head while they watched. The doctors suggested that I be transferred to a bigger hospital the very next day. That night I felt like a part of me was being shut down. I could feel myself shutting down. I was terrified. But my younger brother Evans prayed for me and I lasted till the next day. My mother was given a referral letter and I was discharged from Jinja hospital to Mulago hospital which is a bigger government hospital. My mother had to take me home first and then raise some funds in order for me to be admitted to Mulago.

Disconnected!

When we arrived at the gate of our home compound, I felt a power disconnect me from my body. I saw myself floating above my body as a light. When my mother noticed that I could not move, she called the neighbors to carry me into the house. My mother went to take a shower while the neighbors stretched my body out on the couch. One old lady realized that I was dead and she called my mother out of the bathroom. My mother came to my body covered in a wet towel. She began to pray and to cry out to God on my behalf. When someone dies, they actually hang around their body for around an hour. During this time, it is possible for someone to pray for you and even the doctors can shock the heart and revive a person. When my mother prayed, my spirit, which was in the form of a human heart with light shining around it, re-entered me and my body began to get warm and my bodily systems began to activate and I opened my eyes. As soon as that happened, my mother could not wait for a private vehicle to pick us up and take us to the hospital, so we got on a public bus and my mother paid for the entire row. I was throwing up on my mother from Jinja to Kampala. We went straight to my aunty's house because she is a doctor and she had connections in government hospitals but as soon as we arrived in Kampala, my mother realized that I was cold and stiff. People in the bus began to say sorry to my mother because they could see that I was dead. The house we were going to was across the road so my mother begged some people to help carry my body into the compound.

My Mother's Prayer

While in the compound, my spirit was hanging around my body but my heart had physically stopped beating. By this time, my soul was still in hell being tormented by Satan and his demons. While my spirit was hanging around my body, I saw a very bright light far brighter than the brightness of the sun. The rays of this bright light were calling my name "Erica" and it had some kind of magnet in it which was pulling my spirit and I had my spirit come into full contact with that light I would not have come back. During that time, my mother laid down across my stomach and our navels were facing each other and she said "God I cannot bury my daughter and the dead cannot worship you."

Then through that same bright light came a warm heavy wind that pushed me back into my body and I began to cough. My mother and everyone who witnessed it, was shocked, because they had seen me die. When my auntie who had initiated me came to the house and found me alive, she was not happy. She had hoped that I would die. So she kept on asking my mother, "What did you pray? What did you say?" Surprisingly, God healed me completely at that moment. I never proceeded to the hospital. We just got back on the bus and went home. Had I died in that state, my soul would have remained in Hell forever. I thank God for my mother, her prayers saved my life. I want to encourage mothers to never give up praying for their children even after they die. My mother never gave up on me even after I died, so even if your child is a criminal, keep praying. I have seen a mother's loving prayer save a child from the claws of death itself.

CHAPTER FOUR –
THE SILVER CORD

"Or ever the silver cord be loosed, or the golden bowl be broken, or the pitcher be broken at the fountain, or the wheel broken at the cistern.Then shall the dust return to the earth as it was: and the spirit shall return unto God who gave it."

(Ecclesiastes 12:6,7)

During death, the body has a system which is shut down. Every body part has a cell and a nerve and a vein that is connected to each other. The body has an engine which is the physical heart. The soul and the body are connected through a silver cord. The spirit which is both the spiritual and physical heart is connected to man by God. It is somehow connected to the life-force in our belly and the upper part of our heads which is just above the brain. The human spirit is connected to the brain and the heart. The brain, the heart and the belly are interwoven curiously and when a person is dying they are shut down because the spirit which is the life-force of a man is going back to God who gave it. As soon as the spirit goes, the body begins to decay. The only thing that prevents us from just rotting is the life-force from God that acts as a battery. The belly, the heart and the brain are so very delicate that if they are punctured, a person can easily die. If these three points are neglected in life, one begins to die. (John 7:38)

The Issues Of Life

A man's life flows from the content of his heart. If evil is in the heart, the heart produces a life of evil. But if Jesus lives in the heart, then the heart begins to produce everlasting life. The very life-force of Heaven begins to flow from that heart. In time, the heart can produce the words that have been spoken into it. The word of God can be sown into the heart like seed through meditating and spending time in the word every day. These seeds begin to grow and produce the very promises described in the scriptures. The man begins to live from the inside out, instead of living from the outside in! This is why Jesus instructs us to abide in him and let his word abide in us. The result is the kind of fruit which God wants to see in our lives. This fruit brings glory to God, so when we bear fruit, God prunes us and causes us to bear more fruit.

> *"A good man out of the good treasure of his heart bringeth forth that which is good; and an evil man out of the evil treasure of his heart bringeth forth that which is evil: for of the abundance of the heart his mouth speaketh." (Luke 6:45)*

> *"He shutteth his eyes to devise froward things; moving his lips he bringeth evil to pass."*
> *(Proverbs 16:30)*

The words we speak can bring evil or good to pass.

> *"Death and life are in the power of the tongue, and those who love it will eat its fruit."*
>
> *(Proverbs 18:21)*

This is why we must protect our hearts from poison because if garbage enters into the heart, the heart will multiply that garbage into a lifestyle which pollutes the earth. This is why Jesus said what he did in Matthew 13 verse 24.

> *"Another parable He put forth to them, saying: "The kingdom of heaven is like a man who sowed good seed in his field; but while men slept, his enemy came and sowed tares among the wheat and went his way. But when the grain had sprouted and produced a crop, then the tares also appeared. So the servants of the owner came and said to him, 'Sir, did you not sow good seed in your field? How then does it have tares?' He said to them, 'An enemy has done this.' The servants said to him, 'Do you want us then to go and gather*

> *them up?' But he said, 'No, lest while you gather up the tares you also uproot the wheat with them. Let both grow together until the harvest, and at the time of harvest I will say to the reapers, "First gather together the tares and bind them in bundles to burn them, but gather the wheat into my barn."*

Jesus himself sends the angels to gather the garbage heart producers out of the earth. Eventually, only eternal life producing hearts will be upon the earth. This is the precious fruit production which God desires to see upon the earth. The offspring of intimacy between the word of God and the hearts of men will one day cover the earth as the waters cover the sea.

> *"For the earth shall be filled with the knowledge of the glory of the LORD, as the waters cover the sea." (Habakkuk 2:14)*

The Cord Is Broken

After a person dies, their silver cord which connects the soul to the body is broken and the spirit (God's living dynamo life-force) returns to God and the soul (which is the real you in a spiritual body) either goes to Heaven or Hell, depending on the decision to receive Jesus Christ as Lord AND Savior of your soul or otherwise. You see people are like roads, they can bring you things or take you places depending on who you decide to follow.

> *"Jesus saith unto him, I am the way, the truth, and the life: no man cometh unto the Father, but by me." (John 14:6)*

The name of the Lord Jesus is a mode of transportation for those whose sins are forgiven. His name can transport your soul from point A to point B in a moment of time.

> *"The name of the LORD is a strong tower: the righteous runneth into it, and is safe."*
>
> *(Proverbs 18:10)*

> *"Wherefore God also hath highly exalted him, and given him a name which is above every name, that at the name of Jesus every knee should bow, of things in heaven, and things in earth, and things under the earth and that every tongue should confess that Jesus Christ is Lord, to the glory of God the Father." (Philippians 2:9-11)*

CHAPTER FIVE - HOW I DIED

My early stages of salvation were rough because I was transitioning from the kingdom of darkness to the Kingdom of Light. I had to deal with a lot of character traits and habits that were not of God. I also had to learn how to trust in this new God for everything in my life. I had so many enemies. So many people were looking to kill me. So I was always moving from one home to another. I expected Christians to behave themselves differently than the people of the world but that, unfortunately, was not the case. I was mistreated and many times I was falsely accused of things I had not done. I was oftentimes denied the basics of life like food and clothes and even pads for my monthly cycle.

The first book I wrote about my testimony was taken by a pastor. He even took the authorship and I had no rights over the publication of this book. There were conferences held where I was the main speaker and people were even charged to attend but I was not given any money from the proceeds. I languished in poverty as others profited from my testimony. Despite all of that, I did not stop serving God.

A Ministry Trip Gone Wrong!

One day during the time I was in my second year at Kampala University, I was invited to minister in a village in Mityana district in Uganda. This mission was going to last for a week. For the first time in my life I was not excited about ministry. I was usually quite happy to be invited anywhere to serve the Lord but this time I felt unhappy in my spirit about the whole trip. So I decided to go and pray about it. While I was praying, I heard a voice telling me that I should not go because I would be involved in an accident and that place where we were going was surrounded by death. The place where we were going was deep in the village. A place called "Walumbe Tanda" which means the "tomb of death."

I started praying four days before our trip and the pastor told me that the pastor who was hosting us had just lost his son. His son had climbed a tree to get a fruit and he fell down and died just like that. So I told this pastor that I was not going. But this man insisted that the pastor in the village was counting on us and that we needed to be there for him at that time. Two days towards the conference, another elder lost his son. But this pastor still insisted that we need to go. Two days later as we journeyed, I kept on praying that we would arrive safely. So we did arrive safely. I ministered, I had some gospel songs, so I ministered in music and gave a testimony, in both the conference and the open air crusade. There was another former witch doctor who had given his life to Christ that was also testifying about his conversion to Christ. Both the conference and the crusade were so powerful because we had people giving their lives to Christ. On the last day, the pastor who I had come with, received a phone call that his wife had just miscarried. He requested for me to minister in his place as he was not emotionally stable enough at that time. So I ministered and then I grabbed my luggage because there was only one motor bike available to transport us out of the village to the nearest bus stop.

Accelerating To Disaster

It was getting late, about 7:00 pm, darkness had fallen and we both had luggage which we had overloaded the bike with. There were three of us on this one "boda boda" motorbike including the driver himself. He had also placed one of the suitcases in front of the bike on the handle bars. The roads in that village were rough and full of steep hills. The driver pushed the bodaboda faster and faster approaching 80 kph on a slope headed downward in an effort to save time. The driver lost control, hit a rock and the motorbike overturned. The driver hit his head on a rock and died instantly. I was seated in the middle of the pastor who was behind me and the driver was in front of me. I fell on my knees and began to slide down on my knees against the rough and jagged road. The pastor who was behind me fell on his hands. I was bleeding out of my knees as a result of the fall. Blood was gushing out. The place was dark, nobody could hear or see us. We lay there bleeding for at least an hour before finally another boda boda driver came along and identified us as the people who had just been ministering at the conference.

Going! Going! Gone!

By the time efforts were being made to rescue us, I started coming out of my body. The thing that kills people during accidents often is the sharp pain combined with the fear of what has just happened. I felt pain for some time but the moment fear entered me I started coming out of my body. I could feel myself coming out of myself. Like I was two people in one. I felt like this body of mine was a dress that I was getting out of and I got out of it through my head. So when the people checked they saw that the driver had died but that the pastor and I were still alive. So they decided to rush us to the hospital for treatment. They put us on bikes and rushed us to the hospital. On the way there the pastor was holding my body with his wounded hands. I was running faster than them and beckoning them to go faster because I did not want to die. They took us to one room where they began to nurse our wounds. I was in a lot of pain, I was outside of my body but I could still feel the pain my body was feeling.

After some time as they were nursing our wounds. The doctor called the nurse out of the room. I followed them but they could not see me. I listened to their conversation intently. He asked her to tell the pastor to come out of the room because I was not going to make it. As soon as the doctor said this I began to scream because I could now see two strong hands in the shape of a whirlwind coming to grab me. The pastor was screaming "Erica don't go" while I was also screaming in shock and fear. I went into a dark tunnel. The darkness of this tunnel was darker than any darkness I had ever seen in the earth. The darkness of the spiritual realm is far darker than any darkness in this physical world. That was the last time I saw anything in this physical dimension. The last thing I saw was the pastor screaming and the nurses running to the room with the doctor. Entering into this tunnel was like entering into a mouth. The mouth of death. It was cold, very cold. Like a meat freezer. As you're going through this tunnel, you stop screaming and you begin to gnash your teeth as the fear of it all grips you.

A Cold Dark Tunnel

I could see a very dim light up ahead and I landed on the ground of the tunnel. The force that was pulling me down had slowly come to a stop. This dim light was coming from two gates. One was on the right and the other gate was on the left of this road that seemed to go on forever. I checked out the gate which was on my right hand. I was shocked and terrified at the same time. I saw terrible demons which I had never seen in all my years of serving Satan. These demons were beyond ugly. Grotesquely deformed, and hideous to look upon. They were a hundred thousand times worse than anything you have ever seen in any horror film. These beings were hungry. Very hungry. They growled at me as I peeped through the gate. It's like all of them were waiting for that moment. They thought I was going to fall in the midst of them but I didn't.

One demon had very skinny legs and was barefoot. It's stomach was bulging with extreme malnutrition. It's back was skinny and you could see it's bones. It's neck was skinny and long with ten heads all of which had two sunken eyes deep in the head and jagged teeth sharper than a razor's edge. It's skin was pale grey with greenish reptilian colors. Others were like skeletons. When they're walking you can feel the friction between it's joints as it walks and the claws on its hands were so sharp. These things were not human. Their numbers were too many to count but I did not try to count them.

This gate was a little bit open so I slammed the gate shut and ran to the other gate on my left side. This gate was slightly open. From far away, I could see that this gate was open, but every time I tried to approach and get into this gate I could not fit. It seemed to get smaller in size and I couldn't even fit one of my fingers into that gate. Every time I tried to fit into this gate it shrunk in size. I heard a voice coming from beyond this gate saying "those that call upon the name of the Lord shall be saved." Most of the people who fall into that place are snatched apart by those demons in the right hand gate. Even the ability to say the name of the Lord is a function of your lifestyle while you are still on the earth. Not everyone can see that gate on the left hand side. That gate seemed to use whatever information I had inside me to my own benefit. It was a strange kind of technology that renders to every man what they deserve. When I heard it say "they that call upon the name of the Lord shall be saved" I began to scream "Jeeesuuuuuuuuuus"!! This is the place where people scream the name of their gods. Whatever name you scream is your true god and that name teleports you to the dimension of that being. This is one reason why idolatry is so dangerous. Your god will show up to take you and any deity you can name other than Jesus is a prince of hell. When I called upon the name of Jesus, a very bright light came and struck me and I found myself in a very beautiful place. This place was very bright, pure and full of life! The name of Jesus had teleported me from the place I was between the two gates to this wonderful place.

Jesus!!!!

I was standing on soil that seemed not to make me dirty. I scooped up this soil and poured it on myself and was not getting dirty at all. I scooped up soil and I could see gold and minerals in the soil in plenty. I didn't even need to dig to get this gold, it was just on the surface of the soil. I rolled on this soil back and forth and I didn't get any bruises at all. Not a single scratch. I would jump and throw myself down but I felt no pain. There was an area where I saw stones gathered together and another area where I saw soil and everything was so organized and beautiful beyond description. I saw gardens with all kinds of fruits and there was no trace of corruption or decay. I could tell that there were fruits that had been there for a very long time and yet had never decayed or lost taste. There was not one drop of decay or corruption or deterioration in this place!

The air I was breathing in this place was superior and far sweeter than oxygen. That air is beyond anything we have in this world. The air in Heaven is so pure because the prince of the power of the air is not there to corrupt it. Once you breathe that air you will never die. I was literally breathing in God and exhaling God. I saw four rivers heading in different directions. The source of this water was one spring and the rivers went in four different directions partitioning the land. The place where the four rivers are supplied from is called the river of life.

> "And a river went out of Eden to water the garden; and
> from thence it was parted, and became into four heads.
> The name of the first is Pison: that is it which compasseth
> the whole land of Havilah, where there is gold; And the

gold of that land is good: there is bdellium and the onyx stone. And the name of the second river is Gihon: the same is it that compasseth the whole land of Ethiopia. And the name of the third river is Hiddekel: that is it which goeth toward the east of Assyria. And the fourth river is Euphrates." (Genesis 2:10-14)

This is the river I managed to get to because this place was huge but I could see myself in the reflection of the river's water because this water was far purer than any water I had ever seen. This river is so pure that I could see the details of my own features far better than if I was looking in a mirror on the earth. As I looked at my reflection in this water, I felt like I wanted to drink some of it but as I thought about it an angel spoke to me and said: "No, you cannot drink of this water yet because according to the world you have died but according to Heaven you are not supposed to die yet." Then I turned around to see who was talking to me but this angel was very far from me and yet I could hear him clearly because what I was hearing was his thoughts towards me. As I looked at him he smiled and in a split second he was right in front of me. He was dressed in a white robe with a real silver belt and a golden pair of shoes. This gold and silver was real. Behind him at a distance I could see Cherubim dressed in fine purple robes with silver belts and silver sandals made from real silver. These are servants in Heaven, but they are dressed in wealth. The fine purple was really fine purple. Nothing in this place could compare to anything on the earth. Everything on the earth looked like rubbish compared to this place.

CHAPTER SIX - MY FIRST TRIP TO HEAVEN

At eighteen years of age, God delivered me from the powers of darkness as I elaborated in Erica Part One Seven Years In Hell. I got delivered on a Saturday and began testifying on a Sunday. It has been over thirteen years since I was delivered from the powers of Hell. God began using me to fight the angel of death from the day I got saved. I would find myself positioned in a place where there was going to be an accident. Immediately my spirit would know that this place was going to be ground zero for a tragedy. I would then begin praying and in quite a few occasions I came face to face with the angel of death while on such rescue missions. In all of the missions I have been sent to, nobody has perished though some property has been destroyed. I wrote about one of those incidents in Erica Part One Seven Years In Hell and Erica Part Two Eighteen Years With Lucifer.

I Meet Jesus!

It was in my early stages of ministry that I would get severe attacks from the devil. During these attacks, God began to reveal Himself to me. My full deliverance took three years. During those three years, I was one day under severe attack and while possessed, pastors were praying for me. While possessed I would beat up everyone in the room, so they would tie me up with ropes and I would break them. On one particular night, Jesus entered into the room where I was being delivered and I immediately began worshipping Him. He did not introduce Himself to me but I just knew within myself whom He was. This was Jesus! I had been tormented by all of the demons and the spirits of secular artists who had died but were manifesting themselves through me and I would dance and sing exactly like them. When Jesus stepped in, all of those demons that were tormenting me scattered. I bowed down and began to worship Him. The pastors were amazed by what they were seeing. A person who was possessed one minute ago was now worshipping the Lord Jesus with all of her strength. Then I went into a trance and I was taken into Heaven with Him.

Crossing Over

On our way to Heaven, we arrived at a river where we were supposed to cross over in order to enter into what looked like paradise. Jesus wanted me to be empowered over the marine kingdom which had held me captive for 18 years. But I could not cross over this bridge because I could only see myself sinking into the waters below. Immediately, I began to confess my sins and I started vomiting filthy things out of my mouth. After vomiting everything I was able to cross over the bridge. While I was crossing this bridge, I could hear demons screaming saying "Erica have mercy upon us, don't destroy us."

Then as I crossed, Jesus told me to look down into the waters and I saw Satan in the form of a beast having seven heads and ten horns with leopard skin print. His neck was as long as a giraffe, his feet were like the feet of a bear. Each head had two eyes but they were sunk inside his heads. The color of his heads were like the color of a gecko. He was talking to strange beings like one which was a red serpent having twelve heads and twelve golden crowns on each head. Satan was discussing with these beings and telling them that I had become an enemy and that they should destroy me as soon as possible. Jesus gave me a key and told me that I have power over all the demons and devils that had been tormenting me and that He would be using me to win souls from the kingdom of darkness into His kingdom.

Holy! Holy! Holy!

Jesus took me to a place where the Seraphim are. I saw one seraphim built in the form of a penguin having eyes all over it. This Seraphim were worshipping Jesus and saying "Holy, Holy, Holy, Holy..." and then this same Seraphim began to open the scriptures and quote Psalms 2:

> *"Why do the heathen rage, and the people imagine a vain thing? The kings of the earth set themselves, and the rulers take counsel together, against the Lord, and against his anointed, saying, Let us break their bands asunder, and cast away their cords from us. He that sitteth in the heavens shall laugh: the Lord shall have them in derision. Then shall he speak unto them in his wrath, and vex them in his sore displeasure. Yet have I set my king upon my holy hill of Zion. I will declare the decree: the Lord hath said unto me, Thou art my Son; this day have I begotten thee. Ask of me, and I shall give thee the heathen for thine inheritance, and the uttermost parts of the earth for thy possession. Thou shalt break them with a rod of iron; thou shalt dash them in pieces like a potter's vessel. Be wise now therefore, O ye kings: be instructed, ye judges of the earth. Serve the Lord with fear, and rejoice with trembling. Kiss the Son, lest he be angry, and ye perish from the way, when his wrath is kindled but a little. Blessed are all they that put their trust in him."*

While this Seraphim was quoting Psalms Chapter Two, Jesus' face was shining with more and more brightness and more glory.

While this was happening, my body was quoting the same scripture with the Seraphim, the pastors were watching in amazement while I went from being possessed to worshipping to quoting Psalms Chapter Two in its entirety and yet I had never read that verse. Then I heard Satan screaming and saying, "Erica I beg you, don't destroy my kingdom!" I was so overjoyed to see that the very devil that used to keep tormenting me was now begging me for mercy! Then Jesus told me that if you abide in me and my words abide in you, this devil you see will be nothing before you.

> "Abide in me, and I in you. As the branch cannot bear fruit of itself, except it abide in the vine; no more can ye, except ye abide in me. I am the vine, ye are the branches: He that abideth in me, and I in him, the same bringeth forth much fruit: for without me ye can do nothing. If a man abide not in me, he is cast forth as a branch, and is withered; and men gather them, and cast them into the fire, and they are burned. If ye abide in me, and my words abide in you, ye shall ask what ye will, and it shall be done unto you." ((John 15:4-7))

I saw many Seraphim in that place. Some with eyes all over. Others with ears all over, can hear the cries of children, even infants and interpret their sobs and respond accordingly and give a full report unto the Lord. Others with hands all over and others with tongues all over. They all excel in strength as they fulfill the will of God. Some are in the catering department in Heaven, they taste the food and improve the excellence of taste and smell and sight and each has its own talent and gifting with which it was created. I saw another Seraphim whose feathers were like a blanket and they were comforting spirits. The Seraphim with many eyes are so accurate that they can count how many hairs you have on your head and even the hairs on your body. They are so gifted that they can count the hairs of humanity and number them precisely to the last digit. There are some Seraphim with many lips, they are ministering spirits whose job is to comfort through touching and speaking the word to God's children. Others have ears all over and can hear when man speaks or prays and these carry the words of prayer to God when people pray. There are Seraphim which have shields all over and they shield humanity from attacks of the enemy. The love of God for humanity can also be seen in the attention to detail that God has given for the preservation, sustenance and salvation of His children.

> *"For he shall give his angels charge over thee, to keep thee in all thy ways." (Psalms 91:11)*

Heaven's Hierarchy

The angels minister to the Seraphim. The Seraphim minister to the Cherubim and the Cherubim minister unto God. All of the angelic hosts minister unto God by also ministering unto God's children. When I saw these things, I was speechless. Jesus warned me not to give the pastors I was living with my knowledge because many were not to be trusted. Many had selfish interests and were not interested in helping to build the Kingdom of God but rather building their own empires in Jesus' good name. They would have written books from what I saw and owned them as their own and corrupted something that is sacred and holy and pure. After Jesus showed these things to me, I came back to my body anointed and everyone who was surrounding me (some were possessed) and were delivered instantly and anyone I touched fell down, including the pastors and deacons, etc.

From that day I began casting out devils. My life changed from fearing the devil, to being feared by the devil. I have been a menace to the kingdom of darkness ever since. God has used me to deliver thousands and thousands of souls. The battles have been intense, but by the grace of God, we always win. Glory to the name of Jesus!!

"Behold, I give unto you power to tread on serpents and scorpions, and over all the power of the enemy: and nothing shall by any means hurt you." (Luke 10:19)

Meeting Michael, The Archangel

When I met with Michael, he informed me that every time I fought against him and his armies and appeared to win he had actually let me win. This was part of the strategy of God, to allow me to appear to win battles so that when I would get back to Hell, Satan would see me as one of his champions. This led Satan to not only trust me but to also show me his secrets. Michael told me that the only reason why I survived any battle with him was because of the covenant my parents had made with God. He and all of the angels under his command knew that I would one day serve the Lord. So he had commanded all of the angels under his command not to hurt me. So we laughed about it but when I went to shake his hand, my hand went right through his. He explained that the reason our hands could not meet was because I was not completely dead on the earth. I was taken on a tour of Heaven with the angels. They were showing me how they were preparing a feast, a banquet for the bride of Christ but they were sad that the people they were preparing for were not preparing to meet the groom. They also told me that they feel sad when people don't know who they are and prayer warriors don't deploy them in prayer during spiritual warfare. They explained that they missed the times when they would interact with man and they showed me how Heaven rejoices and a celebration erupts when one soul comes to Christ. They encouraged me to win souls into the Kingdom of God because I am a soul winner. They told me that if I win souls into the Kingdom of God and I stand to defend the vulnerable, poor, and helpless, and walk upright with God, I would be building mansions for myself in Heaven. I asked them if I was in Heaven and they informed me that I was in a place between heaven and earth. So I demanded to see Heaven and to see

God before I came back to my body on the earth. They looked at me with a smile when I asked for this. They are so genuine, so authentic, when they smiled at me, I knew there was no falsehood nor pretense in them. Michael is one of the most friendly and kind beings I have ever met. Very kind to the children of God, but to the kingdom of darkness and it's armies, he is deadly.

Lucifer

Lucifer was transparent with every kind of precious stone embedded in his body. If he would illuminate gold, the entire heaven would shine gold color. If he were silver or topaz or carbuncle the whole heaven would be filled with the light of his countenance emanating from his body.

> "Thou hast been in Eden the garden of God; every precious stone was thy covering, the sardius, topaz, and the diamond, the beryl, the onyx, and the jasper, the sapphire, the emerald, and the carbuncle, and gold: the workmanship of thy tabrets and of thy pipes was prepared in thee in the day that thou wast created." (Ezekiel 28:13)

When Rihanna, the secular pop singer celebrity, is singing her hit single 'Diamonds', if you examine the lyrics she sings, "So shine bright, tonight. You and I, we're beautiful like diamonds in the sky" she is not singing to a man, she is worshipping Lucifer and in exchange for her worship, Satan showers her with the money, power and fame of this world.

When Lucifer was shining, even his eyes would shine gold, silver, diamond, beryl, onyx, sapphire or emerald, and his light would shine brighter than the noon day sun. Lucifer would walk on the stones of fire announcing and heralding the coming of El Elyon. Lucifer would usher in the Presence of Yahweh as He was descending from His throne in the seventh Heaven. As the Lord descended, the glory and the honor and the power of God was so great that no being could ever see His face. All they saw was glory and power and majesty and honor as God passed with the heavenly convoy of the upper echelons of the Cherubim and the twenty four elders. Lucifer would demonstrate great power as he ushered in the presence of God. To see the Lord passing is a spectacle one would never forget. Those who are in Heaven would look up and see the twenty four elders passing and flying before the Lord and bowing and worshipping Him. Lucifer would sing tenor, alto, soprano and bass and all of the human voices and all of the angelic voices at the same time. He did not need any background vocals or choir or any additional assistance from musicians or a band or a symphony. On his right hand he has six wings and on his left another six wings. Lucifer was perfect until evil was found in him and he fell.

In his wings on the right hand were percussions and drums and bass and other instruments of a superior technology to anything we have ever seen on the earth. On the left hand side, the three upper wings are the stringed instruments, harps, acoustics, bass guitar, violin, and other stringed instruments I had never seen before and have never seen since. The lower three wings on his left hand side were horned instruments. Trumpets, trombones, saxophones, clarinets and every horned instrument known to man and others yet unknown. When it came to dancing, there is no being who could dance better than him. He could dance and sing and produce instrumentation for himself simultaneously. Lucifer was perfect in beauty.

When it came to dressing, if Satan was doing reggae, he would look like a reggae artist, if it was hip hop, he would change into hip hop clothing and appear like a rapper and so forth. Lucifer's nails are usually black, he always liked them to be black and red. Lucifer could also add the sounds of animals to his voice. Lucifer

could imitate every animal sound imaginable. God created Lucifer to be able to speak and every creature could hear him. Because
Lucifer was a Cherub, he also had the ability to change into any
of the four faces of the other Cherubim. The image of man was
created out of one of the major faces of God which is the face of a
man.

CHAPTER SEVEN – BACK TO HEAVEN I GO

The following day I was taken to church. While the pastors were praying for me I fainted. I was rushed to a nearby hospital. While I was in that state, many tests were being performed on me. God took my spirit to a place where people who die before their time go to. That place is hidden between the physical and the spiritual worlds. Between where I was and where that place is, there is a glass that separates us. I was not fully dead, I was just unconscious.

The Wealth Of The Kingdom

This Cherub told me that Satan is raising an army of humanity to fight against their own Heavenly Father, but God is determined to protect man's inheritance and continue with His plan for man's redemption. Then this Cherub showed me the wealth of this land. All of the precious metals, natural resources, and rare earth metals are on the surface of the land. No digging required, no sweating, no corruption, no decay, no death. All of the animals and wildlife in that place is peaceful. The lions were playing with goats and the wild animals were playing with each other. There is complete peace!

In Between Heaven And Earth

I asked the angel where we were. He replied that this is the place which connects the spirit and the physical worlds together. When you leave the physical world, there is a realm between the spirit and the physical dimensions. This world is called Eden. The angel who was explaining these things to me was a Cherub. He told me that he was the Cherub that sent Adam and Eve out of Eden and stood guard to prevent them from partaking of the tree of life. The Cherub told me that God loves to come to this place because He still comes to Eden to meet with man. Man is still on the heart of the Father. God shows up to meet with man till this very day, but man does not show up to meet with God. God still shows up in Eden in the cool of the day to fellowship with man because that is how committed God is to man.

This place where God comes to meet with man is called Eden. The holy place was called Eden before Adam and Eve fell from the presence of God. Till this day, the Father desires to meet and fellowship with His children in the cool of the day. This Cherub is the same one who pushed Adam and Eve out of the garden of Eden so that they could not take of the tree of life. This same Cherub will usher man back into the garden when man is ready.

The angel told me that there are people who die before their time. Some through abortions, others through sacrifices, and others through accidents. These souls are caught between the two worlds until their actual time of death. The Cherub showed me where they are. I could see them filing petitions to God because of the people who were responsible for their untimely death. Even Abel, the righteous brother of Cain went there to file a petition against his brother Cain for murdering him. While these souls are there awaiting their transportation to either Hell or Heaven depending on their choices while they were alive, the Cherub allowed me to see the transportation which takes these souls to their final destination. One mode of transportation was what looked like a flying saucer or a flying plate which spins while releasing fire from it's edges to ward off unwanted visitors. When it came down, it opened it's doors and stairs came down like the stairs used to board an airplane. Two very strict looking angels who do not blink their eyes guarded either side of the stairs. The angel Gabriel stepped down with a list in his hand ticking next to the names of every soul whose name appeared in the list. The souls whose names were in the list seemed to know that they belonged in this flying machine.

One thing amazed me, I saw a mother and her daughter who both died in a car accident. The Cherub who guarded this place showed me how the mother and daughter died in an accident. The flying machine came and the daughter boarded as Gabriel congratulated her. The girl's mother remained behind because her name was not in the book. The girl had given her life to Jesus Christ. She tried again and again to share the love of Christ to her mother but she loved this world too much. She was wealthy and did not see the need for having Jesus in her life. When she died, she could not qualify to go where her daughter was going. She was headed for hell. She had refused to make Jesus her Lord and Savior. She had died and never had a chance to change her character before her silver cord broke. Her character was set, she would be exactly who she was (character wise) when she died, for eternity.

> *"Know ye not that the unrighteous shall not inherit the kingdom of God? Be not deceived: neither fornicators, nor idolaters, nor adulterers, nor effeminate, nor abusers of themselves with mankind, Nor thieves, nor covetous, nor drunkards, nor revilers, nor extortioners, shall inherit the kingdom of God." 1 Corinthians 6:9,10*

Another man left his wife and his two children and waved at them while he boarded the flying machine. I asked the Cherub why the husband would not warn his family about the place where they were headed. The Cherub (whose name is Fierce) told me that even if he warned them, they would not take his word seriously, the same way they would not listen to him preaching the gospel of Jesus Christ while they were still alive. Once a person dies, their character and personality remains intact. After angel Gabriel welcomed them, he waved at us and I was so excited. Then the aircraft took off spinning with flames spreading on every side.

Heaven's Landscape

I saw four rivers in the garden and the fish of the rivers are peaceful and happy. Adam used to swim and enjoy with the crocodiles and travel in huge fish and cross into various dimensions. Adam could fly with birds, he did not need airplanes.

I saw where the tree of the knowledge of good and evil was located. The place is surrounded with darkness. Angels armed with swords of fire are guarding that place. I went back in time and saw how Eve fell. She was not even supposed to be in that area nor enter into that place where the tree of the knowledge of good and evil was located. When Eve went and ate of the tree of the knowledge of good and evil, Adam saw that she had fallen and was stuck in that place and he knew that if he ate of the fruit, God would redeem him, but if he left Eve there, she would have been stuck on her own in that place until this day. What Adam did was redemptive.

> "And Adam was not deceived, but the woman being deceived was in the transgression."

> (1 Timothy 2:14)

When God saw that Adam had sinned, He sacrificed animals for them immediately and covenanted to eventually redeem them. God replaced the clothing which Adam and Eve had made for themselves which were garments of shame and instead gave them sacrificial garments of redemption which were prophetic in naturebecause the blood of the lamb would eventually redeem them from their sins. God's plan of salvation had been played out right there in the garden with Adam and Eve.

CHAPTER EIGHT - THE WITCH DOCTORS ARE WAITING

One day I went to minister in a small gathering of witch doctors in eastern Uganda. I was a baby Christian but my desire to serve God made me agree to go. When I arrived, I found about thirty six witchdoctors gathered in a small building. I started with praise and worship with the small group of people we had gone with. Then I gave my testimony and gave an altar call and sixteen witch doctors gave their lives to the Lord Jesus Christ. I began casting out devils from the rest of them and they surrendered their witchcraft. This mission was very powerful. On my way back to where we were supposed to spend the night, I died. By the time my body arrived at the place where we were supposed to stay the night, I was dead. During that time as we traveled back, my aunty who had been tormenting our family with witchcraft as I wrote about in Erica Part Three Witchcraft & Spiritual Warfare, had gone to a shrine in South Africa and she wanted me dead. They had filled a basin with water and the witchdoctor had been calling my name and waiting for my image to show up in the water so that they could cover my spirit and suffocate it in water so that I would die and my soul would be enslaved by the marine kingdom. My aunty was calling my name through a mirror in the same shrine. This was so that when I showed up in the mirror, she would pierce my image, I would instantly die and my soul would be enslaved to her. During that time, my spirit had left my body but I was giving them a hard time because I would not show up in the water basin or in the reflection of the mirror. All they could see was a shadow of someone running from place to place inside the darkened shrine.

I Die Again!

Meanwhile, the people I was with physically began to panic because they did not know what to do or what to tell my parents because I was unresponsive. They began to walk around the car praying for me and crying out to God for about four hours. The nurse had confirmed that I was dead, so they did not see the need to rush a dead body to the hospital. They just felt the burden to pray. As they prayed, the angel of the Lord struck the witchdoctor and he collapsed. My aunty began to attend to the witchdoctor and call for an emergency ambulance to carry him to the hospital. I could even see the city where they were bewitching. She was in Durban, South Africa, seeing a sangoma for the purpose of killing her own niece. This angel which was sent had a huge chain which he used to bind all of the demons which had been responsible for my death. Then he carried me and placed me back in my body and did surgery on me for my body to function again. As soon as my body began to function, the angel tapped me on my forehead and said "Don't fear child, it is well, I'm going to put your enemies where they belong." Then I saw Him proceed with His mission, swinging His chain seeking the enemies of the children of God. When our hosts saw that I was alive and my eyes were open, they quietly carried me to the house and they began to give me warm water with a spoon. They were massaging my body because I had been stiff. As they massaged my body with a warm cloth, the blood began to circulate again and as I became warm, my blood began to flow again. This process took about 3 hours. They gave me warm soup to drink but I could feel every drop as it entered into my stomach. After this process they took me outside and poured warm water on my body and dressed me up and decided to send me to Kampala the same night in order to avoid the traffic jam but their real reason for sending me away the same night was because they were scared. They did not want me to die in their hands.

My Third Death

On our way to Kampala, they called my mother and told her to meet us in Jinja town and then proceed to Kampala. On our way to Kampala, I died again, this time, in the hands of my mother. I was taken to a relative's house and they started praying for me. This time I could see my aunt in another shrine in South Africa desperately trying to kill me again using a charm shaped in the form of a doll made of fiber. She wanted my spirit to enter into that doll so that she could strangle me once and for all. As she was doing her witchcraft, my mother and other relatives had put me on the floor and they were praying for me. Then the angel of the Lord came and hit my aunty and the witchdoctor. They collapsed, then He took me out of that shrine and He kept on chaining all of the demons which were responsible for my death.

CHAPTER NINE
- THE TRAIN

I heard loud music and booming airbase coming from a train that was decorated with all kinds of disco lights and half naked women, snakes and dragons spitting fire. There were coffins and chains, half naked men and as soon as the train approached the boarding station, God the Father turned His back on these people as they danced and sang along to the hit song "Celebrate Good Times, Come On!" These people entered into the train without a moment's hesitation. They were doing everything that was in their character to do while they were alive. Some were smoking weed, others were even having sex on the train and doing drugs while others were fighting and some were busy stealing, cursing, and speaking evil.

> *"Then shall two be in the field; the one shall be taken, and the other left." (Matthew 24:40)*

All Aboard!

After everyone had made themselves comfortable on the train, the doors shut and the train began to move. I saw Satan sitting at the back of the train, hiding his face. I saw some men dressed up as bishops with briefcases full of people's money. They had holy anointing water and oil which they were selling on the train. They had bodyguards and appeared like very important religious men. People were break-dancing like Michael Jackson on that train and the train began to pull off. The music changed to another song by the rap artist Ludacris "Move b**** get out the way, get out the way b***** get out the way . . ." As the train left, Fierce told me that this is how they lived their lives while they were still alive. "This is the path they chose, the path that leads to destruction." I watched as the train went out of sight and the music faded into the screams of people terrified as they landed in Hell and God had turned His back on them. It was too late to turn back. Satan was now fully in charge of their souls.

I was horrified by what I saw. I knelt down and listened to the screams of the damned. The Cherub helped me back up on my feet and God descended from the hill and He walked towards us and He said that He created everything including man and the angels and He gave them a will. He cannot decide for them. They either choose to obey and live or disobey and die. Then He showed me His hands. His hands were full of His works. They were not soft hands like ours. Everyone of us left a mark in God's hands when He was creating us. All of the animals, the plants, the birds, the insects, the animals, the angels, the heavens and the earth and even mankind are all the workmanship of His hands. Then I put out my own small hands and said, "Do I have any works so far/" He then looked at me and laughed and said "No." Then He encouraged me to create something with my hands that He could bless. So ministers and lovers of God should not be lazy, because our Father in Heaven does not just sit on the throne of Heaven. He works!

> "But Jesus answered them, My Father worketh hitherto, and I work." (John 5:17)

> "The heavens declare the glory of God; and the firmament sheweth his handywork."

(Psalms 19:1)

When Moses saw the burning bush, it was God Himself that showed up in the bush because God is a consuming fire Himself.

"For our God is a consuming fire."

(Hebrews 12:29)

Time Stands Still In The Fire

When God crosses into the physical world, it means that eternity has stepped into time. Therefore, time bowed the knee and stopped for Him. The bush was not consumed because fire takes time to burn. But if fire was frozen in time as eternity crossed into the physical dimension, the bush could only catch fire, but could not burn because chronos time had stopped. When Moses stopped to look at this bush he was looking at God and the voice which spoke to him was the voice of God. When I saw God, I saw a man who appeared to be flames of fire. His facial features are like ours but with a pure white beard and white eyebrows and even His eye lashes were white for He is the Ancient of Days and has always been and always will be. His teeth were the most perfect teeth I have ever seen. The whites of His eyes were perfectly white but the pupil of His eyes are pure fire. This is the same God who showed up in the midst of the fiery furnace with Shadrach, Meshach and Abednego. Again He stopped time as He entered into the physical dimension and not so much as a hair on their heads smelled like smoke.

> *"And the princes, governors, and captains, and the king's counsellors, being gathered together, saw these men, upon whose bodies the fire had no power, nor was an hair of their head singed, neither were their coats changed, nor the smell of fire had passed on them." (Daniel 3:27)*

Fire cannot burn fire. If anything, the fire of earth was worshipping the God of all fire in the midst of the fiery furnace.

> *"And of the angels he saith, Who maketh his angels spirits, and his ministers a flame of fire." (Hebrews 1:7)*

This verse in Hebrews actually comes from Psalms 104:4

> *"Who maketh his angels spirits; his ministers a flaming fire:"*

David understood these things long before he died. God used to show David dimensions of the spirit and as he worshipped, the Lord would reveal more and more. David saw as God created the Heavens and the earth. Psalm 33:6 was prophetic eye witness testimony, not just a psalm.

> *"By the word of the LORD were the heavens made; and all the host of them by the breath of his mouth."*

John the revelator was dipped in boiling hot oil and exiled on the isle of Patmos. It was after dying to this world and being ready to pour out his life, that he began to interact with the higher dimensions where God is calling His sons. For me to see what I saw, I had to die. No flesh shall glory in God's presence.

> *"That no flesh should glory in his presence." (1 Corinthians 1:29)*

No Flesh!

The flesh is listed in Galatians 5:19-21 as:

> *"Now the works of the flesh are manifest, which are these; dultery, fornication, uncleanness, lasciviousness, idolatry,*

witchcraft, hatred, variance, emulations, wrath, strife,
seditions, heresies, envyings, murders, drunkenness, revel-
lings, and such like: of the which I tell you before, as I have
also told you in time past, that they which do
such things shall not inherit the kingdom of God."

In order to ascend into the dimensions where God wants His sons, the flesh must die and the Spirit of God must find expression instead.

"Who shall ascend into the hill of the Lord? or who shall
stand in his holy place? He that hath clean hands, and a
pure heart; who hath not lifted up his soul unto vanity,
nor sworn deceitfully. he shall receive the blessing from
the Lord, and righteousness from the God of his salvation.
This is the generation of them that seek him, that seek thy
face, O Jacob. Selah." (Psalms 24:4-6)

May God raise up sons who are ready to die to self and live unto Christ.

"And they overcame him by the blood of the Lamb, and by
the word of their testimony; and they loved not their lives
unto the death." (Revelation 12:11)

Dying to self is the key to living limitless in the Kingdom of God.

"For the earnest expectation of the creature waiteth for the
manifestation of the sons of God." (Romans 8:19)

All of creation is waiting for the sons of God to begin manifesting because creation knows that when the sons of God manifest, the corruptible nature of the world will be reversed into incorruptible immorality. The Adamic fall will have been rectified and creation will obtain the liberty from slavery to Satan which they have patiently awaited for millennia. For this to happen, the church must enforce the finished work of the cross.

Repent Or Suffer The Consequences!

Then as I was approaching my body with this angel, he gave me a message for one of my aunties who was expecting a child. He said that the kingdom of darkness has sent an attack against her and her baby but she has empowered the kingdom of darkness by the way she is treating people. Instead of creating wars with people she should pray for her health and her baby's health and create peace with people. When I told her that message as soon as I entered my body she did not take my message seriously. Her baby died soon after. This aunty used to mistreat people and speak insultingly to people. I told her that every time she insulted people, the child developed deformities in the heart. By the time the child was born, it had a cleft lip and a hole in the heart. The baby died.

When the sins of mankind were placed on Jesus at the cross, the consequences of sin, which included sickness, disease, poverty, oppression, curses, infirmity, depression, misfortune, affliction and every other sentence for crimes committed (sin) were settled. This is why during evangelistic crusades, the sick are healed, the blind receive their sight, the deaf begin to hear, the dumb speak and demons are cast out and people are set free from all manner of curses and affliction because Jesus paid the price for us all so that we could be free and come back into union and communion with the Holy Spirit of God. The case of sin against the sinner has been satisfied, there is no more legal ground for the disease to stay. So it has to go. When the sickness leaves, they are healed.

CHAPTER TEN - THE GATES OF HEAVEN

I was taken to a very peaceful area with flat land. This area had streets that had glass but below the glass there was silver and gold and from where I stood, I looked above me, and there were steps descending down to where I was. There were seven steps with seven gates and each step had a gate. One step was comparable to the distance from the surface of the earth into the Heavens. There were angels guarding each gate. There was music from all of the Heavens, worshipping God. Some of the songs I heard were like the songs we used to hear, here on earth. I asked Fierce why they were singing the songs we sing on earth. He replied that the authentic worship songs that we sing actually come from Heaven. These songs are given to worshippers who repeat them on earth and the angels sing along as we worship. One of the songs they sang was "Bless the Lord, oh my soul, and all that is within me bless His Hoooooolyyyyyyyy Naaaaaame!" I was so happy, it was then that I realized that all this time we had been interacting with Heaven even though we were on the earth. I had no idea that we sang the same songs and interacted this closely with Heaven.

Gate One - The Guardians

The next thing I heard was the sound of thousands of footsteps, like the sound of armies marching. Then a portal opened above us and I heard the sound of a very loud trumpet, and I saw angel Gabriel blowing this trumpet. Then I saw the angel, whose name was Fierce, opening gates in Heaven. When Fierce opened the first gate which opens the other gates, I saw angels which have eyes all over their bodies. These angels do not smile; they do not blink; they look like iron - real iron - no bullet can pass through them. They were the color of pure iron; they are metallic. They are in the shape of human beings. They are giants. These beings guard the gates of Heaven and they are colossal in size. These beings are so tall that if their feet were to touch the surface of the earth you could not see their faces because of the sheer height of them. They do not talk, they do not smile, their eyes are sharper than any technologically advanced camera lens. There was another set of angels covered with noses and their sense of smell is so developed that they can smell anything and everything coming into the atmosphere of Heaven. Another was covered in ears. Their hearing is at such sensitivity that they can hear vibrations, thoughts, feelings, whispers, etc. These beings can hear the thoughts of those in Heaven and were involved in casting out Lucifer and his rebellious angels as they conspired to overthrow the throne of Heaven.

No Illegal Entries

Michael also told me they are in charge of security. He said they are there because many beings have been trying to enter into Heaven illegally. So these beings are there to secure the gates of Heaven and establish the territorial integrity of the gates and entrances of Heaven. I saw other angels covered with mouths all over them. When God came down to see what mankind was doing during the time of Nimrod in Genesis 11. He saw that the whole world was of one language and one mind and He knew that they would succeed at whatever they put their mind to if they were united. So God in His wisdom sent one angel with mouths all over and this angel began speaking and sending vibrations into all of the people and they began speaking different languages and this is how God confused the languages of the men of the world during Nimrod's day. Google has an application that translates other languages. Translating apps are simply attempts at trying to rectify the problem which this angel created as it obeyed the commandment of God. Then the Cherub Fierce told me that for any human being to enter there, they must be found completely innocent of any and all tendencies of the flesh. These tendencies are listed in Galatians 5:19-21

> *"Now the works of the flesh are manifest, which are these; Adultery, fornication, uncleanness, lasciviousness, idolatry, witchcraft, hatred, variance, emulations, wrath, strife, seditions, heresies, envyings, murders, drunkenness, revellings, and such like: of the which I tell you before, as I have also told you in time past, that they which do such things shall not inherit the kingdom of God."*

Fierce said that the only way a person can be purified was through the blood of Jesus. If it were not for the blood of Jesus, no human being would qualify to enter into the gate of Heaven. The security forces would catch them and disqualify them based on established precepts and laws which can never be changed.

After seeing these angels I was allowed to pass through the main entrance. As I passed this gate the angels that guard it did not even budge, they faced directly ahead of them. They are so serious about their integrity that nothing can distract them. Nothing at all!

They Barely Made It

When I saw the Heavens opened, it was an angel that opened the first gate and inside the first gate, I saw very many people. This place was crowded. These were people who gave their lives to Christ but barely survived Hell. Some had just given their lives to Christ on their deathbeds. Others were unfaithful believers who reconciled to God shortly before they died. I had an opportunity to speak with one of them who told me that he had died around two thousand years ago. He told me that he had been begging God for a chance to go back to the earth and do what he was supposed to do but his prayer has been in vain. He told me that this place was beautiful but I deserved better. He said, "Since you have an opportunity to go back where you came from, go and fulfill your purpose so that you can inherit a better place here."

The Second Gate - Saved But Complacent

Then the gate to the second Heaven was opened. I saw christians who did not want to go deep into the things of God here, but they were saved. At their places of work, nobody knew that they were saved because they were shy about their salvation. They always wanted to be prayed for, they could not stay in prayer for even half an hour. In their opinion, someone who prayed for over an hour was being overly spiritual. They were commercial christians. When they died, they were put in the places where they were comfortable in Heaven, not too close to God but then again, not too far away. Most of the people I saw there were pastor's wives. They thought that because they were the pastor's wife they did not need to seek God for themselves and be close to Him. They enjoyed their positions of leadership in church, but in many ways they were still carnal. They wielded power as the "first lady" of the ministry and enjoyed the fame but they were not close to God. The second Heaven was their portion.

The Third Gate - Pastors And Bishops

An angel opened the third gate. These gates were the extent that one could see into the Heavens. In the third Heaven, I was able to see very many pastors, including many who we hear about in Christian literature and some of the generals we read about in christian history books. They had huge ministries, properties, resources and big names. These ministers were from Asia, Europe and Africa. They were also begging God for a chance to come back to the earth and do their work as they were supposed to do it. Their requests in this regard were also denied.

A Bishop's Regret

I remember one minister whose name was Ben who was shouting at the top of his lungs telling me to remind his wife how they began with just a desire to serve God. He was apologizing for not being a good example to her. He was telling me to tell his wife (who is still alive) not to take people's tithes and offerings for her pleasure because there is a greater reward in Heaven which he missed and he did not want her to miss it.

The angel began to explain to me that when this man Ben started ministry he was very humble. He just wanted to serve God. But afterwards he was corrupted. He began taking money from the vulnerable and building mansions and posh vehicles and shopping for his wife overseas. He owned properties and even a private jet at the expense of the poor whom he could have helped. Towards the time of his death he repented for his greed, and this is how he made it to Heaven but without a reward. He left his reward on earth, his name is recognized in the earth as one of the generals of his time. The church still remembers the impact he had but, unfortunately, he had a smaller reward than what he should have received. This man should have been with king David and Abraham, Isaac and Jacob, the patriarchs and the like. But vanity robbed him of a greater reward in Heaven. The third Heaven was his portion, and he wanted me to tell his wife the truth. A few years after this encounter I actually met his wife at the burial of the Archbishop Silas Owiti In Kisumu, Kenya, East Africa. She had come to attend the burial. I was looking forward to giving her the message but what I saw her doing shocked me.

She was seated at the VIP section of the podium during the burial with the other archbishops. They were clad in the red and white garments of bishops with gowns around their shoulders and priestly collars around their necks and the mitre hat with the open top similar to what the catholic bishops wear. She actually looked like a Catholic Bishop. She was seated at the front row on the altar/podium facing the congregation. Her assistant was seated directly behind her and because it was hot in Kisumu, her assistant was fanning her with a handheld fan like one of the Pharaohs in the days of ancient Egypt on a hot summer's day. Her assistant's skirt was too too short and too tight, the congregation could see her thighs from where the audience was seated. This bishop would send her assistant to fly to Europe to buy her new clothes so that she could change her wardrobe every few months. Her fingers were covered in gold rings.

I did not get a chance to speak to her and tell her the message from her husband but I pray that I will have an opportunity to do so one day. I hope the ministers that are reading this remember that there will be a time of accountability to God for their opulence. Just because you came from the ghettos and the slums when you began ministry does not justify spending millions on luxurious purchases while God's children are starving and wallowing in poverty. It is those who God has blessed financially who refuse to live in opulence and remember the poor and have mercy on them despite the fact that they also came from poverty who lay up for themselves treasures in Heaven unimaginable. They have a special place in the heart of the Father and their humility, self sacrifice and selflessness has granted them rank and stature among the immortals of Heaven forever. Such men cannot be found in the third Heaven. Such men are found with king David and the patriarchs in the upper rankings of Heaven. Amen.

The Fourth Gate - Faithful Servants

I stood with Fierce the Cherub of the Lord and gazed as another guardian angel opened the fourth gate of Heaven. Inside the fourth gate of Heaven were men and women who had stood with the work of the Kingdom of God. They were among the intercessors who would pray for the body of Christ, they were faithful, they loved the Lord, they invested heavily in the Kingdom. Their resources were for the Kingdom not themselves. They were living a fulfilled and colorful life in Heaven. But even among these there were many who were pleading with God for the opportunity to come back to the earth in their bodies and preach the gospel because of the need. They spoke to me and told me, "Now that you have the opportunity to go back, go and serve the Lord and fulfill your destiny. Do not rest, until the day you have breathed your last breath, because you will have plenty of time to rest in Heaven."

The Fifth Gate - The Real Generals Of Heaven

Another angel opened the fifth gate of Heaven. Inside the fifth Heaven, I saw the real generals of Heaven. People who were persecuted for the Kingdom. Among the people whom I saw was a very old lady but looking strong and beautiful compared to the old people we have here on earth. Her sight was perfect. Her memory was excellent. She was living in a mansion, one of the biggest in the fifth Heaven. It was made of fine gold, silver, diamond and precious stones. Angels were always at her service. Fierce enabled me to go back and see what this woman did in her days on the earth. This woman died about one hundred years ago. She used to clean her church in her country Zimbabwe. Her name was Monica. Monica used to clean the chairs and the toilets in the church. She also used to mop and clean the offices and windows. She was a widow who had no children of her own. She would make a living by working in people's land and from the money she would make she would bring in her tithes and offerings and she would help the poor with the money left over. This woman cleaned the church faithfully but was never paid. Everyone else who worked there was paid but she would not be paid. She worked faithfully for free. She would also intercede for everyone who would sit in the very chairs she washed and cleansed faithfully. One day she fell so ill and the church did nothing to stand with her, nobody visited her, when she failed to come in to clean, the administration of the church quickly paid a replacement to do her job. This replacement could not even do half of the work this woman was doing, but he was being paid. When she recovered, she still went back to church and worked with her replacement faithfully. Two months after this, she fell very ill and died. A few church members went for her burial but the pastor did not even attend. She was buried in a public cemetery with no earthly honors to speak of. But the moment she died, she was welcomed to Heaven in glory and honor. She is known in Heaven as one of God's great generals. There is no one in Heaven who does not know Monica because her mansion is one of the biggest in the fifth Heaven. It has her name written on it with all of the precious stones.

The Sixth Gate - Patriarchs And Matriarchs Of The Bible

The angel of the sixth Heaven opened up the gate and I fell on my face. The brightness that came from that place put me down. The first person I saw there was Abraham, the father of faith. I saw Noah, Enoch, and Israel whose name was Jacob until the Lord changed it. I saw king David with his harp standing before a huge choir of real worshippers who were also men and women who lived here on the earth and worshipped faithfully and made it to Heaven. Everyone of them had their own instrument. They were all generals in the Kingdom of God.

I saw Paul and Peter. I liked Peter because he is still talkative jovial and everyone in Heaven is fond of him. Even the angels love him. Adam and Eve were also there.

Sarah, Abraham's wife, Mary and Joseph, even Lazarus whom Jesus raised from the dead and the other Lazarus the poor man who died and was carried into Abraham's bosom. This man is still in Abraham's bosom in the sixth Heaven because when he lived, though he was poor, he always gave glory and honor to God. Zacheus, the tax collector, and so many others. All of the faithful heroes of the Bible were there with mansions and their names written on their mansions and their works were there with them. The mansions are built by works, but salvation is not earned by works. Only mansions are built by works. There is a grace that teaches your soul through laboring in the Kingdom. This grace impacts your soul with the Holy Spirit character for Kingdom living. The only thing you will carry with you from the earth is the immortal personality that you trapped in your soul. That is what you will carry with you into eternity.

> *"And I heard a voice from heaven saying unto me, Write, Blessed are the dead which die in the Lord from henceforth: Yea, saith the Spirit, that they may rest from their labours; and their works do follow them." Revelation 14:13 KJV*

CHAPTER ELEVEN - THE SEVENTH HEAVEN

When the angel of the seventh gate was about to open the gate, Cherubim flew above us and they were drawing curtains. One layer was gold, the other layer was silver, the other layer was fine purple and the other one was white. These were thick curtains as thick as the clouds of the earth. Even Fierce the Cherub who was guiding me bowed down and everything that was alive from the sixth Heaven all the way down to the first began to bow down. The only ones who did not bow down were the seraphim angels who were guarding the entry points of Heaven. These warrior angels kneel on one knee and place their right hand over their heart and their other hand before them at an upward angle holding their weapon. They bowed themselves in a manner that allowed them to remain on duty and still show honor and reverence to The One who sits upon the throne of Heaven.

His Name Is Holy

As the Cherubim drew the curtains, they heralded and pronounced accurately all of the names of God in every human language and tribe and tongue.

El Elyon (The Most High God, Genesis 14:18-20),

El Shaddai (Lord God Almighty, Genesis 17:1),

Yahuah Adonai (Lord Master, Genesis 15:2)

Yahuah Elohim (God of Power and Might, Genesis 1:1)

Yahushua (Jesus, Matthew 1:21)

Yahuah Rapha (The Lord that heals, Exodus 15:26)

Yahuah Nissi (The Lord my Victory/Banner, Exodus 17:15)

Yahuah Jireh (The Lord will Provide, Genesis 22:13,14)

Yahuah Mekoddishkem (The Lord who Sanctifies You - Leviticus 20:8)

Yahuah Roi (The strong One who sees, Genesis 16:13,

El Olam (The Everlasting God, Isaiah 40:28-31)

Yahuah Raah (The Lord my Shepherd, Psalm 23:1)

Yahuah Sabaoth (The Lord of Hosts, Isaiah 1:24)

Yahuah Shalom (The Lord is Peace, Judges 6:24)

Yahuah Shammah (The Lord is Present, Ezekiel 48:35)

Yahuah Tsidkenu (The Lord Our Righteousness, Jeremiah 23:6)

Qanna (The Lord is a Jealous God, Exodus 20:5)

Yahweh (Lord, Yahuah, Deuteronomy 6:4)

This is when I realized that He has many names and deeds but He is one God. Every name opened a different dimension of God. Each name has power in it to do as His name describes.

All Creation Bows Before Him

Now after the protective curtains had been drawn, and the names of God had been proclaimed to all of His creation including some human beings on the earth who hear what is happening in Heaven and they bow even though they are on the earth. I saw the animals on the earth bowing and the lions roaring and the elephants raising their trunks like trumpets and the giraffes raising their necks and jumping up and down. The zebras were bowing their heads and raising them up, the dogs would not stop barking, the hens were cooing, the cows were raising their heads and mooing, babies were smiling but the mothers did not know why they were smiling. The birds went out and began to sing in every sound while they were displaying their abilities in reverence and honor in both Heaven and earth. All of the beings in the oceans and the seas and the rivers and the lakes would dive into the water and bring out their heads in total surrender to the one who created them. As they dived it meant "Without You, we are dead," then as they rose it meant "With You, we are alive." The monkeys, chimpanzees and gorillas began shaking the stems of the trees by jumping from one branch to another telling every insect in the bushes and the forests to worship the King of Kings as they leaped from one tree to another. Then the insects began to release sounds and the frogs and the lizards raised their heads in surrender to the King of Kings. Then the snakes began to coil themselves in a circle and lift their heads in surrender to the one who is on the throne. The wind began to blow to the north, the south, the east and the west in order to cause the plants and the trees and the flowers and all of the plants to bow in all angles in loyalty and reverence to the King. The sun bowed unto God and sent it's rays directly to the throne and the moon gave the brightest half of its light to the throne and the other half to the earth because it was on duty (as it was during the night that I died) but it was surrendering to its Creator.

The stars began to produce a sound of drums in a spectacular manner. They shined their light onto the earth and then into Heaven. The waters and the seas, the rivers, and the lakes of the earth began to flow greatly in specific directions and then collided in order to produce the sound of many waves and then they combined their sound with the sound of the stars of heaven which were drumming. Then the eagle began to ascend higher and higher and then descend over and over and over again. Then the clouds formed and assembled and released lightning and thunder and the earth opened its mouth and swallowed the lightning from the clouds as a sign of total surrender. Then the mountains shook and the rocks began to roll down onto the other rocks and collide with them in surrender unto Him who sits between the coals of fire.

David Plays The Harp

Then king David the psalmist began to play his harp. It must be noted that before David became a king he was a worshipper who kept the sheep of his father, Jesse. It was during these times of worship that David grew in intimacy with Yahuah Raah (The Lord, my Shepherd Psalms 23:1). It was this Cherub by the name of Fierce who taught David. David was singing unto the Lord by himself while he was taking care of his father's sheep. Then Fierce approached him while he was in the form of an ordinary man and told him that he sings very well but there are dimensions he can go to with a certain instrument.

Then David asked him, "which instrument, what is an instrument?" David didn't even know what an instrument was. So Fierce taught David how to make this instrument and David made it. David asked, "What should I call this instrument?" Fierce replied, "A harp," then he left him. David struggled to learn how to play this instrument for quite some time. As David struggled to play this harp, Gabriel the Cherub came and showed him how to play the harp and how to utilize this harp to access spiritual dimensions and usher in the presence of God. Gabriel also gave David a list of songs to sing from Heaven. Then David mastered the harp, and would play skillfully and the angels would come and dance to his music. Fierce was impressed by what he saw David doing and he came and taught him how to use the sling in warfare. By the time David was fighting Goliath, he had been properly trained by Fierce who is like the Lord's personal bodyguard. Though God is all powerful, He has Cherubim that excel in strength as they obey His command. David and Fierce became close. Fierce (under the command of the Lord) taught David how to play songs of war.

> *"Blessed be the Lord my strength which teacheth my hands*
> *to war, and my fingers to fight:"*
>
> *(Psalms 144:1)*

This is why when David would play, the demons that were tormenting Saul would leave him for some time. Fierce taught David how to make the harp speak.

> *"And it came to pass, when the evil spirit from God was*
> *upon Saul, that David took an harp, and played with his*
> *hand: so Saul was refreshed, and was well, and the evil*
> *spirit departed from him." (1 Samuel 16:23)*

In Heaven, before the throne of the Lord, David played skillfully just as he did on the earth and the worshippers of Heaven played their instruments at their best. Meanwhile Solomon, the son of David gave poetic and proverbial words of wisdom.

The Twenty Four Elders

The twenty four elders, twelve on one side and twelve on the other side, two by two on each step of the six steps of Heaven (so four on each step on either side all the way up to the sixth Heaven). Then on the seventh step where the gate of the seventh Heaven is, on the right hand stood Abraham, Noah and Moses. On the left hand was Israel, Adam and Joseph (Jesus' stepfather). While these men were bowing themselves and worshipping at the seventh gate, there was also Elijah, Elisha and Ezekiel prophesying to the nations. As they prophesied there were other great prophets standing besides them, Aaron (one of the very handsome prophets, whose beard was spoken of during the process of being anointed with oil Psalms 133:2), Samuel, Jeremiah, Isaiah, Amos, Habakkuk, and many more. Just after the gates were open on the inside I saw John the baptist dressed as he was on the earth with the skin of an animal holding a small trumpet announcing the glory of the King of Kings.

The Women Of God

Now just on the left hand side of John there were women like Eve (the mother of all living), Mary the mother of Jesus, Sarah, Elizabeth (the mother of John the Baptist, Jesus auntie), Mary and Martha (the friends of Jesus, they are still His friends till this day and forever), Rahab (former prostitute and grandmother of Jesus) Naomi and Ruth, Hannah, Mary Magdalene, Esther (the Queen still wearing her crown), the mother of Solomon, Bathsheba among the queens of Israel, even the old widow (of Mark 12:42) who gave all she had was very rich in Heaven. The woman with the issue of blood was there worshipping and giving glory and honor to the King of Kings and the Lord of Lords. Women are recognized in Heaven and have rank and stature, so don't let anyone tell women that just because you're a woman you cannot serve God. That is a lie, serve like the other women who served and are now in Heaven giving glory to God. They served the Lord in humility and are rewarded forever.

There were too many heroes of the Bible to name. Even some who are not written in the scriptures but they are there, in Heaven, they obtained eternal life. May the grace of God help us to reach that place. Then I saw Enoch kneeling before the throne of the Father.

CHAPTER TWELVE - THE FOUR FACES OF GOD

God has four faces. The face of a lion, the face of an ox, the face of an eagle and the face of a man. He has the ability to transform into a rushing mighty wind. A dove is a symbol of God's character, love, humility, intimacy, kindness, faithfulness, patience, perseverance, gentleness, long suffering and mercy. A dove is one of the most harmless birds in existence. It is the only bird which has no bile or gall. Bile is bitterness. There is no bitterness in God.

The Face Of A Man

The face of the Cherubim is the face of a man, with all of the features of a man and all of the five senses. The reason the Cherubim also have the face of a man is so that the Cherubim may interact with man on man's level. In most cases when God is sending a message to man He uses Cherubim like Gabriel, Michael, Raphael or Uriel and others. All of the angels are named after God. Michael or Gabri-el named after some of the names of God, El Elyon (God most High) El Shaddai (God Almighty) etc.

These Cherubim relate very well with man. They can be seen by man, they talk to man, the can speak any language from any nation of the world fluently. They can transform to appear like any nationality. When they appear in the form of a man, they appear very attractive looking. In Genesis 19, the two angels who came to Sodom were Cherubim. Michael the archangel is a Cherub, Gabriel is also a Cherub, even Lucifer was a Cherub (but could also function in the office of the seraphim). Lucifer's name meant "light bearer." Light represents knowledge. Cherubim are clear like water in color, they only appear to men if they want to or if they are on a mission from God. Otherwise they can move like the wind and operate just out of the sight of mankind.

Despite everything that the angels, the seraphim and the Cherubim can do, they still admire mankind and wonder, what is it about man that has God so excited? None of these other beings, with all of their abilities to carry out different functions in the Kingdom of God is above man. Out of all of the beings in creation, only man was created in the image of God and in His likeness. Man is a co-creator with God. The fallen angels need the minds of men in order to create things otherwise they are not creators. God dwells in unapproachable light. None of His creation has ever seen His face. Before the creation of mankind, this problem still existed. Elohim needed a way of allowing His creation to understand Him without Him needing to scale down His glory or change Himself because anything God does has a profound effect on His creation. If Elohim were to change Himself, all of creation would also change. Yahweh needed a way to express Himself to His creation. Yahweh does not change. So God the Father communed with God the son and God the son communed with God the Holy Spirit in the pleasant koinonia of the community of the divine. This blessed fellowship of the Godhead resulted in the formation and the creation of man. The aim of Elohim was to solve the problem of His creation not knowing who Yahweh is and to expand His Kingdom into dimensions of existence previously non-existent and thus unexplored. There was no point of reference. Nothing with which to compare God to. Of all of the billions of species created by God, who were worshipping Him and glorifying Him and praising Him in perfect harmony, nothing even came close, in comparison to Him, nothing that is, until the creation of man.

> *"What is man, that thou art mindful of him? and the son of man, that thou visitest him? For thou hast made him a little lower than Elohim, and hast crowned him with glory and honour. Thou madest him to have dominion over the works of thy hands; thou hast put all things under his feet:" (Psalms 8:4-6)*

Even the angels and the seraphim and the Cherubim wonder about man. Who is man, that almighty Elohim would go out of His way to die for him in order to redeem him. None of the angels who fell were offered redemption in this manner. Why the special treatment? Why does God love man above all else? This love ignited jealousy among the hierarchies of the celestial beings before Adam fell. This love for man created a revolt in Heaven. Lucifer already wanted the place and position of God. For God to create another species and crown him with glory and honor and then place him above Lucifer and above all of God's creation, was just too much for Lucifer's pride to bear. Till this day, Satan is fighting for this position. Satan wants everything that God gave man. He hates man with a passion. To him, man is the only thing standing in the way of his ambitions for greatness.

The Face Of A Lion

Behind those Cherubim was another group of Cherubim dressed in white robes, silver belts and golden shoes. These Cherubim have four faces. The face of an ox, the face of an eagle, the face of a lion, and the face of a man. They can display all of the faces at the same time or one face at a time. Those Cherubim were able to display all of the faces that they had and they gave me confidence in the armies of Heaven. When they display the face of the lion, they are very fierce. No demon would dare go near them, including Satan himself because when they put on the face of the lion, they wear one of the faces of God and when they roar, the sound that comes from them does not bounce back like an echo. It is a weapon that breaks every wall and every obstacle or mountain that lies ahead of God's children. The face of the lion represents boldness. It possesses the spirit of leadership, grace, dignity, stability and power. It also expresses royalty, kingship and greatness. When the lion roars, it catches everyone's attention, God has placed it's fear in all other life forms. When it roars, everything shuts down and pays attention. The office of the lion is the office of the apostle. An apostle simply means "sent one." But this sent one is no ordinary person.

> *"The wicked flee when no man pursueth: but the righteous are bold as a lion." (Proverbs 28:1)*

The vibrations possess the power to break down the elements of atomic structure. Matter is no match for them! There is power in sound when it comes from the children of God. When the children of Israel besieged the walls of Jericho in Joshua 6:20 it was the shout of the people combined with the roar of the Cherubim that brought the walls crumbling down.

> *"So the people shouted when the priests blew with the trumpets: and it came to pass, when the people heard the sound of the trumpet, and the people shouted with a great shout, that the wall fell down flat, so that the people went up into the city, every man straight before him, and they took the city." (Joshua 6:20)*

The Cherubim roar as God roars because as they are roaring they are acting on orders from God and they are also protecting the children of God. If God were to just roar, everything in the earth would crumble to dust and powder. So the Cherubim actually scale down the power to an appropriate size and scale. Otherwise the roar of the lion of the tribe of Judah would be an extinction level event.

> "And one of the elders saith unto me, Weep not: behold, the Lion of the tribe of Judah, the Root of David, hath prevailed to open the book, and to loose the seven seals thereof." (Revelation 5:5)

God sends the Cherubim on specific missions to act on His behalf and the Cherubim function with the power of God. Through species like the Cherubim, God finds expression in other dimensions. Then the Cherubim displayed the face of an eagle. This is a face of flight, precision, courage, boldness, strength and patience. This is why the scripture says:

> "But they that wait upon the Lord shall renew their strength; they shall mount up with wings as eagles; they shall run, and not be weary; and they shall walk, and not faint." (Isaiah 40:31)

God can also appear in the form of a Lion. When the book of Revelations calls Him the Lion of the tribe of the tribe of Judah, it is not just being poetic.

> "And one of the elders saith unto me, Weep not: behold, the Lion of the tribe of Juda, the Root of David, hath prevailed to open the book, and to loose the seven seals thereof." (Revelation 5:5)

The face of a lion is a face of power! When God manifests that face and He roars, even the devil, Satan, who roars, "like a lion," is put in his rightful place. When the Lord roars, all of the principalities, the powers, the rulers of the darkness of this world and the spiritual wickedness in high places, bow! The face of a lion, is the face of judgement. It also symbolizes His authority over all of His creation. When Daniel His servant was cast into the lion's den, God the Lion roared and all that the lion could see of Daniel was the Lion of the tribe of Judah. They kept their distance and bowed before Daniel who was in the image and likeness of God because he was a secret place dweller. A man of prayer. A man of spiritual stature and rank. A man of conviction and unshakeable integrity. A man of the altar. A man who would seek the face of God daily. A man who fasted twenty one days until Heaven could break through the enemy's ranks in the second heaven and deliver the message of a change in regimes from the empire of Persia to the empire of Greece which would bring humanity a step closer to the end of the age. His name is forever inscribed in the halls of eternity, because he stood for God in his day and raised a standard of Godliness for the children of God to emulate. This shows us that the only things you can carry through the gate of eternity are the things you worked out in the earth, by the way of the Spirit.

As the king's soldiers were casting Daniel into the lion's den, Daniel was shouting as any normal man would, but God was roaring through Daniel's voice and the sound was that of a man but the vibrations were that of the Lion of the Tribe of Judah. The pride of lions in the den bowed in reverence to the God who manifested through Daniel, His faithful servant.

"I in You, and You in me, Yod Heh, Vav, Heh, Yod He-Sheh Vav Heh" Yod-Heh-Vav-Heh (YAHWEH)

By Pastor Danladi Hassan

> *"By the time Darius the king received the decree to be signed by his presidents and princes, to establish a royal statute and make a firm decree that whosoever shall pray to any God or make any petition to anyone except the king Darius for a period of thirty days, shall be cast into the lion's den. The plot had already been hatched from the prince of Persia against Daniel because he was threatening his position. Believers need to know that when they live Godly lives, in the midst of an unGodly world, they set off vibrations that upset the equilibrium of iniquity in the land. These vibra-*

tions are capable of toppling a prince of darkness from his throne and bringing mankind one step closer to the rule of the King of Kings and Lord of Lords. King Darius was not a very spiritual man, he had no idea that his princes and presidents were writing a decree that would result in Daniel being made a law breaker. As Daniel was judged by the prince of Persia (the principality that ruled behind Darius the king), the prince of Persia was judged by the Lion of the tribe of Judah, the prince of peace roared, and that was the end of the reign of the prince of Persia. The princes and presidents who wrote the decree as they were commanded by their idols, were also judged and cast into the den of lions with their entire families, and children and wives who had been in covenant with their idols. This marked the end of the idols who ruled under the prince of Persia for the king Darius was converted and made a royal decree throughout all his empire that no other God was to be worshipped except the God of Daniel. What a way to leave your mark in the earth!"

"Then king Darius wrote unto all people, nations, and languages, that dwell in all the earth; Peace be multiplied unto you. I make a decree, That in every dominion of my kingdom men tremble and fear before the God of Daniel: for he is the living God, and stedfast for ever, and his kingdom that which shall not be destroyed, and his dominion shall be even unto the end. He delivereth and rescueth, and he worketh signs and wonders in heaven and in earth, who hath delivered Daniel from the power of the lions." Daniel 5:25-27

When God manifests the face of the Lion, He is dealing with territories, principalities, powers of darkness and the spiritual rulers of this world with the face of judgement. When the rulers of darkness had come through the men who had come to arrest Jesus they asked for Jesus of Nazareth, he replied, "I am He" and they all fell backwards on the ground. Jesus just gave himself up to them but they did not take him by force. Jesus allowed them to take him because the time had arrived for him to crush the spirit of death once and for all. Jesus was not concerned about mere mortals, he had bigger fish to fry.

The Face Of An Eagle

The eagle devours serpents which is a form of Satan. It does not fight with serpents on the ground. It takes them up into the air and begins to feed on them in the air. The eagle takes the serpent out of its natural habitat. It can choose to drop the serpent from great heights or simply start taking bites out of it. Either way, the serpent is no match for the eagle. Taking the serpent up in the air is the strategic position of prayer for the believer. Jesus said we should always pray.

> *"And he spake a parable unto them to this end, that men ought always to pray, and not to faint;" (Luke 18:1)*

The place of great power, great strength, great grace, great ability, great dominion, lofty heights and total victory is the place of prayer. The eagle does not fly away from storms, it uses the momentum of the storm to rise to levels of altitude far above its own natural ability. Every storm is your opportunity to rise to new heights previously unattainable. The female eagle will test the male eagle with a stick during courtship to test its ability. The female will fly and allow the male to follow her, then she'll drop the stick and the male will dive and catch the stick and bring it back up. This process may repeat several times as the female tests the male. The male is being vetted because this is the same process the female uses to teach the young eagles how to fly when their wings have formed. The female will drop the young eagles and they are forced to flap their wings or die. The male will catch them if they are not ready to fly and bring them back. The raising of the next generation is an eagle-like character because it takes foresight to raise the next generation. At a certain age (usually forty years) the eagle finds a cleft in a cliff or a high place. It goes through a process of losing its feathers to the very last one as others grow. After this stage of renewal, the eagle can fly higher, see further, live longer, and additional forty years are added to it. The eagle understands the language of self sacrifice.

The eagle is prophetic in its office and can spot sin from very far away. A real prophet should be able to spot sin in the church and expose it to the light of day which is the Word of God. May the Lord use this publication to give you an eagle's character traits as you serve Him. Many of God's children are entangled in the bonds of immorality, because Satan knows that they have the eyes of the eagle, but immorality blinds the eyes. So he sends spirits of immorality to blind them, like Samson.

The face of an eagle is a face of strength and patience.

> *"But they that wait upon the Lord shall renew their strength; they shall mount up with wings as eagles; they shall run, and not be weary; and they shall walk, and not faint." (Isaiah 40:31)*

One of the servants of God who walked in this dimension was Elijah. And Elijah passed on this mantle to Elisha. Elijah told Elisha that if you see me going, you will get what you asked for. What Elisha had asked for was a double portion of Elijah's anointing. This required great patience on Elisha's part. Unfortunately, the same could not be said for Gehazi, who went running after Namaan the Syrian to fulfill the lust of the eyes. When Gehazi went after him, Elisha's spirit followed after him in the dimension of the eagle. He saw everything Gehazi did. As a result of Gehazi's greed and desire for selfish gain, the leprosy of Naaman the Syrian did cleave to him and to his seed after him.

> *"The leprosy therefore of Naaman shall cleave unto thee,*

and unto thy seed for ever. And he went out from his presence a leper as white as snow." (2 Kings 5:27)

Many years later during the years that Christ walked the earth, this same lineage of lepers could be found outside of the walls of Jerusalem. The desire for selfish gain robbed Gehazi of the office of the prophet after Elisha. Conversely, Elisha's anger robbed him of a successor who would have carried a double portion of Elijah's anointing and helped Israel defeat her enemies through a long succession of seers with the patience and the eye of the eagle.

The eagle does not fight the serpent on the ground, it takes the serpent up into the sky and in so doing, changes the battleground. Then the eagle releases the serpent into the sky. The snake has no stamina, no power and no balance in the air. It is useless, weak and vulnerable, unlike on the ground where it is powerful, wise and deadly. Take your fight into the realm of the spirit through prayer and when you are in the spirit realm, God takes over your battles. Never fight the enemy in his comfort zone, change the location of the battlefield like the eagle and let God take charge through your earnest prayer. You will be assured of clean victory.

> *"Confess your faults one to another, and pray one for another, that ye may be healed. The effectual fervent prayer of a righteous man availeth much." (James 5:16)*

> *"And he spake a parable unto them to this end, that men ought always to pray, and not to Faint;" (Luke 18:1)*

The eagle also mates in the air, it does not mate on the ground like chicken. Any Christian who does not live a life of prayer is like a chicken. Chicken are easy prey for serpents. Anytime someone goes to pray, it is a time of intimacy, intertwining your DNA with the DNA of God. Moses spent so much time in the presence of God that by the time he came down from the mountain he did not even realize that his face was shining and the children of Israel could not steadfastly look upon his face.

> *"And it came to pass, when Moses came down from mount*
> *Sinai with the two tables of testimony in Moses' hand,*
> *when he came down from the mount, that Moses wist not*
> *that the skin of his face shone while he talked with him."*
> *(Exodus 34:29)*

Moses had spent so much time in the place of prayer, that God quickened his DNA and had changed him into a God-man. This is the only kind of person whom God can trust with the powers of the age to come. Moses had been so changed in the presence of God, that had God never commanded him to do so, he never would have died. God did not just desire for Moses to be changed in His presence. God desired for all of the children of Israel to ascend into the mountain just like Moses. It was their fear that prevented them from ascending into the mountain. They feared because of the sin that was in their lives.

> *"Then they said to Moses, "You speak with us, and we will*
> *hear; but let not God speak with us, lest we die." (Exodus*
> *20:19)*

Had the children of Israel been pure in heart, they would have all entered into the mountain and into the presence of God like Moses and all of their DNA would have been changed into the image and likeness of God. They would have transcended death. They would have been alive till this day, stronger than ever. But the evil of their hearts separated them from God and instead of becoming God-men, they died in the wilderness. Many Christians are like these children of Israel. They do not want the deep things of God. They want the pastor, prophet, teacher, spiritual father to go for them. As a result, they never ascend to the mountain top, they're preoccupied with the things of this world, and they die in the wilderness of vanity.

> *"Who shall ascend into the hill of the Lord? or who shall
> stand in his holy place? He that hath clean hands, and a
> pure heart; who hath not lifted up his soul unto vanity, nor
> sworn deceitfully. He shall receive the blessing from the
> Lord, and righteousness from the God of his salvation. This
> is the generation of them that seek him, that seek thy face,
> O Jacob. Selah. (Psalms 24:3-6)*

When Jesus needed additional encouragement during his hour of
trial in the garden of gethsemane He took Peter, James and John
with Him to pray. As He prayed, they fell asleep. This is also
how the church behaves. When it's time to pray, they are sleeping. Sleeping can mean many things, chasing after promotions at
work, or striving to be a millionaire or a billionaire. Anything
time consuming that pulls you away from seeking the presence of
God in intimacy can put you to sleep to what really matters. Car-
eers have been designed to replace intimacy with God in the secret place. The secret place is where the appetites for the things of
this world are replaced with hunger for God. As you come to God,
He begins to deal with your appetites until your only desire is the
thing that pleases Him. It is in this place where one learns to walk
in the Spirit. Not just by regular attendance at church, but time
sacrificed and invested in the secret place with God.

> *"He that dwelleth in the secret place of the most High shall
> abide under the shadow of the Almighty." (Psalms 91:1)*

This hunger can increase to the point where the deep things of
God become your craving and your portion and your life becomes
a manifestation of the in workings and the out workings of the
glory of God.

> *"If you are taught how to walk in the Spirit and you attend
> and service those burdens very well, those burdens will lead*

to the place of encounter. When burdens come to you, the first thing you should do is to align and service that burden by the Holy Ghost. Stay in the place of prayer, until the possibilities, the instructions and the mandate are clearly given to you, that is when you can be an effective witness. Witnessing is a projection of the working of the inner life. It's not the strength of the dexterity of your speech, it's a function of the supply of the Spirit, and only men whom the Holy Spirit has worked Himself into can provide witness." -Apostle Mike Orokpo

This is a life of bearing much fruit. Witnessing is a function of fruitfulness. The opposite of this is sleep. Those who sleep cannot pray and those who cannot pray cannot witness. The dangers of sleeping can be seen in Matthew 13:24-30

"Another parable put he forth unto them, saying, The kingdom of heaven is likened unto a man which sowed good seed in his field: BUT WHILE MEN SLEPT, his enemy came and SOWED TARES among the wheat, and went his way. But when the blade was sprung up, and brought forth fruit, then appeared the tares also. So the servants of the

householder came and said unto him, Sir, didst not thou sow good seed in thy field? from whence then hath it tares? He said unto them, An enemy hath done this. The servants said unto him, Wilt thou then that we go and gather them up? But he said, Nay; lest while ye gather up the tares, ye root up also the wheat with them. Let both grow together until the harvest: and in the time of harvest I will say to the reapers, Gather ye together first the tares, and bind them in bundles to burn them: but gather the wheat into my barn."

The tares which the enemy sowed are the words which the enemy used to entice humanity to seek intimacy with the things of this world instead of the things of God. By seeking the things of this world, they lack the foresight of the eagle. The foresight of the eagle can see that one hundred and twenty years of human life is but a drop in the ocean compared to eternity. Many "churches" lack the DNA of God. These are not ministries which were born out of a place of intimacy with God, but were rather born out of a place of intimacy with the god of mammon, which produces a strong desire for the things of this world which are soon passing away. These "sow a seed for God to meet your need" prosperity churches have over emphasized one part of the Kingdom at the expense of all of the others.

> *"And why are you worried about clothes? See how the lilies and wildflowers of the field grow; they do not labor nor do they spin [wool to make clothing], yet I say to you that not even Solomon in all his glory and splendor dressed himself like one of these. But if God so clothes the grass of the field, which is alive and green today and tomorrow is [cut and] thrown [as fuel] into the furnace, will He not much more clothe you? You of little faith!*
> *(Matthew 6:28 AMP)*

God does not demand a seed before He provides for you. He provides for you because He loves you and because He is Yahuah Jireh, the God who provides. It is a dimension of His character encapsulated in His Name. By learning and internalizing this aspect of God, all your needs are met. Adam did not fall from needs and wants, he fell from glory. You cannot be a child of God and fail to operate in power, and fail to cast out devils and fail to pray for the sick and preach the gospel. Standing for the gospel of the Kingdom takes courage.

> *"Have not I commanded thee? Be strong and of a good courage; be not afraid, neither be thou dismayed: for the Lord thy God is with thee whithersoever thou goest." (Joshua 1:9)*

During the times of the storms of life, the eagle will patiently study the storm, it examines the source and the direction of the storm. Then it wisely calculates it's trajectory and ascends to heights previously unattainable in ordinary weather. It is at altitudes above the level of the clouds, an eagle whose eyesight has dulled with age will stare at the sun, which only it can do. The sun's rays burn away the mist of age and its sight is renewed once again.

Is your sight getting blurry in these last days? Look to the Son, so that the mist of time spent elsewhere can be burned away, and your spiritual sight can be renewed once again.

"Looking unto Jesus the author and finisher of our faith; who for the joy that was set before him endured the cross, despising the shame, and is set down at the right hand of the throne of God." (Hebrews 12:2)

"Hearken to me, ye that follow after righteousness, ye that seek the LORD: look unto the rock whence ye are hewn, and to the hole of the pit whence ye are digged." (Isaiah 51:1)
"

But we all, with open face beholding as in a glass the glory of the Lord, are changed into the same image from glory to glory, even as by the Spirit of the Lord." (2 Corinthians 3:18)

It is a spiritual law, that whatever you gaze at, you will become. The eagle also goes through a process called molting, where their old feathers fall out and new feathers replace them over time. This is a gradual process whereby lost feathers are renewed gracefully.

"Who satisfies your mouth with good things, So that your youth is renewed like the eagle's."

(Psalms 103:5)

The Face Of An Ox

The other face of the Cherubim which I saw was the face of the ox. An ox possesses great power. It represents supply, increase, provision, multiplication and generosity.

> *"Where no oxen are, the crib is clean: but much increase is by the strength of the ox." (Proverbs 14:4)*

The ox is seen in 1 Kings 19:19 with the prophet Elisha:

> *"So he departed thence, and found Elisha the son of Shaphat, who was plowing with twelve yoke of oxen before him, and he with the twelfth: and Elijah passed by him, and cast his mantle upon him." (1 Kings 19:19)*

The ox is a power agent - an asset of increase. The office of the ox is the office of the evangelist. The evangelist is an agent of the harvest of God. The evangelist points people to the cross of the Lord Jesus Christ because it was at the cross of the Lord Jesus Christ that the wrath of almighty God was satisfied, for Christ took our punishment for sin and the judgement for all of the sins of mankind was placed on him for our sake.

> *"All we like sheep have gone astray; we have turned every one to his own way; and the Lord hath laid on him the iniquity of us all."*
>
> *(Isaiah 53:6)*

The face of an Ox is also a representation of multiplication, fruitfulness, subduing, increase and dominion. The face of an Ox is also a representation of supply and wealth. This is why the Bible says:

> "But my God shall supply all your need according to his riches in glory by Christ Jesus."

> (Philippians 4:19)

When God created Adam, he blessed him and commanded him saying,

> "And God blessed them, and God said unto them, Be fruitful, and multiply, and replenish the earth, and subdue it: and have dominion over the fish of the sea, and over the fowl of the air, and over every living thing that moveth upon the earth." (Genesis 1:28)

God wanted Adam to be His representative on the earth. In the hierarchy of all of creation there is first of all God, then Man and then the rankings of the angelic host. When we speak of the Ox, we speak of increase, we speak of power, strength and dominion.

> "Where no oxen are, the crib is clean: but much increase is by the strength of the ox." (Proverbs 14:4)

> "Behold now behemoth, which I made with thee; he eateth grass as an ox. Lo now, his strength is in his loins, and his force is in the navel of his belly. He moveth his tail like a cedar: the sinews of his stones are wrapped together. His bones are as strong pieces of brass; his bones are like bars of iron. He is the chief of the ways of God: he that made him can make his sword to approach unto him." (Job 40:15-19)

The Ox is hardworking, there is no laziness in him. He hates laziness, he plows the field with great strength. Cattle are also in the family of the Ox. In marriage, it is customary for the man to give dowry to the father of the bride as a sign that the man who is taking this daughter is capable of taking care of her and is also hardworking. No father would like to give his daughter's hand to a poor, irresponsible or lazy man. It is easier to tempt a poor person than a rich one in areas of wrongdoing for gain. God expects His children to be productive and use their hands to work to bring increase just as He does. God works and work was never a curse. Work predates the fall of Adam. Genesis one shows God working to build His creation.

"But Jesus answered them, My Father worketh hitherto, and I work." (John 5:17)

When Jesus found a tree which had no fruit he cursed it:

"And Jesus answered and said unto it, No man eat fruit of thee hereafter for ever. And his disciples heard it." (Mark 11:14)

"Every branch in me that beareth not fruit he taketh away: and every branch that beareth fruit, he purgeth it, that it may bring forth more fruit." (John 15:2)
"

Be patient therefore, brethren, unto the coming of the Lord. Behold, the husbandman waiteth for the precious fruit of the earth, and hath long patience for it, until he receive the early and latter rain." (James 5:7)

"And the man Jeroboam was a mighty man of valour: and Solomon seeing the young man that he was industrious, he made him ruler over all the charge of the house of Joseph." (1 Kings 11:28)

It is Godly and vital that we teach coming generations, congregations and ministers that work is of the Lord and in work there is dignity. The mindset of hard work instilled into future generations will create a bright and prosperous future. Ministers should work and preach.

> "In the morning sow thy seed, and in the evening withhold not thine hand: for thou knowest not whether shall prosper, either this or that, or whether they both shall be alike good."

> (Ecclesiastes 11:6)

In Ecclesiastes 11:6 we see that God's word says that ministers should continue in both areas of work (ministry and business) so that if one is slow the other can compensate for the shortfall until the other catches up. I recommend that you read my husband's book "The Truth About Money," for an inside look at work, the church and money. It is available on Amazon Kindle. A well balanced perspective and wisdom will help clear up any confusion in this area.

> "Through wisdom is an house builded; and by understanding it is established: And by knowledge shall the chambers be filled with all precious and pleasant riches. A wise man is strong; yea, a man of knowledge increaseth strength."

> (Proverbs 24:3-5)

> "He called ten servants of his, and gave them ten mina coins, and told them, 'Conduct business until I come."' (Luke 19:13) World English Bible

The Ox is also the representation of the office of the evangelist as previously stated concerning the four faces of the Cherubim. The Cherubim have four faces like God because they are His representatives in some of His dimensions. But man can carry more dimensions of God than the Cherubim. This is the closeness of God and man represented in the menorah.

In the menorah, the three candles on either side of the middle candle add up to six which is the number of man. The candle in the middle represents the Lord. So in total the number is seven which is the number of completion. The entire symbol represents the intimate fellowship of God in man. This special relationship with the Creator is only shared with man. No other creation of God shares this closeness with divinity. This is one major reason why the kingdom of darkness hates humanity so much. If God loves man this much, then we owe it to Him to live for Him and live a life of self sacrifice that God's will may be done through us. Sacrifice is crucial because the first thing sacrifice brings is authority. This is because authority is needed to advance His Kingdom. God wants people who can give up things to secure authority so that the Kingdom can move forward. The first thing sacrifice does is to confer authority. Men, by sacrifice of their own desires and ambitions, consecrate themselves unto God. The bullock and the ram and the lamb are all in the family of the Ox.

In 1 Chronicles 29:21 says,

> "And they sacrificed sacrifices unto the Lord, and offered burnt offerings unto the Lord, on the morrow after that day, even a thousand bullocks, a thousand rams, and a thousand lambs, with their drink offerings, and sacrifices in abundance for all Israel:"

The dimension of the Ox also symbolizes the area of sacrifice. It works hard now in exchange for a better tomorrow. It pays the price for the greater good. It is unselfish, generous, powerful and yet gentle.

> "Unto Adam also and to his wife did the Lord God make coats of skins, and clothed Them." (
>
> Genesis 3:21)

God was operating in the dimension of the Ox and in so doing He was promising them that He would deliver them from the fallen state which they were in. Indeed, Jesus came in the dimension of the Lamb of God which took away the sins of the world.

> "*The next day John seeth Jesus coming unto him, and saith, Behold the Lamb of God,*

There is far more detail to be discovered in all of the faces and dimensions of God. It is up to you to hunger and desire for Him and to abide in Him until He begins to reveal Himself to you.

CHAPTER THIRTEEN - THE THRONE OF GOD

I only saw one throne in Heaven. He is God the Father, God the Son and God the Holy Spirit. His throne is built in such a way that it ascends beyond the Heavens, it only descends when He desires to be with His creation and address them. When He ascends there is a place He goes where no created being has ever gone. It is above the sides of the north. The day Lucifer tried to ascend there, he was cast down into the earth, into Hell, to the sides of the pit (Isaiah 14:12-15). That was Lucifer's judgement for just thinking about and attempting to go into that hallowed place. I advise anyone with Heavenly ambitions, don't ever think of ascending above God unto the sides of the north. Know your level, fear the Lord and worship Him who is the only one worthy of such glory and honor and praise. Amen.

The Seven Spirits Of God

Before the throne of God I saw seven spirits. These are the seven spirits of God in Isaiah 11:2

> *"And the spirit of the Lord shall rest upon him, the spirit of wisdom and understanding, the spirit of counsel and might, the spirit of knowledge and of the fear of the Lord".*

These seven spirits are

1) the spirit of the Lord

2) the spirit of wisdom

3) the spirit of understanding

4) the spirit of counsel

5) the spirit of might

6) the spirit of knowledge and

7) the spirit of the fear of the Lord.

We see a type of these same seven spirits of the Lord in the book of Esther chapter one when king Ahasuerus who reigned from India to Ethiopia threw a feast in Shushan. This was the palace where his princes, servants, and nobles sent his seven chamberlains to call Vashti the Queen to come to the feast so that the royals of his kingdom could see her beauty. But Vashti was holding a party of her own in the palace of the king Ahasuerus for the women of the realm.

> "On the seventh day, when the heart of the king was merry with wine, he commanded Mehuman, Biztha, Harbona, Bigtha, and Abagtha, Zethar, and Carcas, the seven chamberlains that served in the presence of Ahasuerus the king, to bring Vashti the queen before the king with the crown royal, to shew the people and the princes her beauty: for she was fair to look on. but the queen Vashti refused to come at the king's commandment by his chamberlains: therefore was the king very wroth, and his anger burned in him." (Esther 1:10-12)

So the seven chamberlains (are a type of the seven spirits of God) that were sent to call the queen Vashti (who is a type of the church who are proud and busy having their own programs aside from the program of intimacy which the King desires). The seven spirits of God are calling the bride into a place of intimacy with the King.

> "And I beheld, and, lo, in the midst of the throne and of the four beasts, and in the midst of the elders, stood a Lamb as it had been slain, having seven horns and seven yes, which are the seven Spirits of God sent forth into all the earth."
>
> (Revelation 5:6)

The seven spirits of God have been sent into the earth to call the bride into the place of intimacy with God. The place where their lamps will be filled with oil until they run over (Psalms 23:5) in preparation for the coming of the groom (Matthew 25:1-13). The wise virgins seek the Presence of God and abide there waiting for Him (Psalm 91:1). It takes time to prepare the virgins for the King. This is the time of purification which the seven chamberlains will have with the bride to be, before the consummation of the wedding. Before the marriage supper of the Lamb, is the time where the bride makes herself ready. It is the seven spirits of God who help make the bride ready.

> "Let us be glad and rejoice, and give honour to him: for the marriage of the Lamb is come, and his wife hath made herself ready." (Revelation 19:7)

The foolish virgins are busy chasing the world like Vashti. They never had the heart of the King, and the King never had their hearts.

The Trumpet Sounds

Now when John the Baptist blows his trumpet, the twenty four elders who are standing on either side of each of the six stairs, two by two, they begin to fly in opposite directions, blowing trumpets and exalting the throne of God. In other words as these elders are flying of their own accord and worshipping and blowing their trumpets, the throne of God ascends into unapproachable light and the prophets begin to speak the mysteries of the Kingdom. It is when God is being exalted that the spirits of the prophets are able to ascend with the throne of God and they begin to speak the mysteries of the Kingdom and the mind of God. Meanwhile king David is playing the harp quietly while Solomon is speaking proverbially the secrets of the dimensions of the realms of the spirit. Then David begins to sing and worship and with every stroke of his harp he moves the heart of God from His place of exaltation. David's worship combined with the stroke of his harp, strikes a cord in the Spirit and brings down the Presence of God again. Worship can open dimensions in the heart of God to bring down His presence. Worship can cause God to stop whatever He's doing and pay attention to you. Men were given the area of worship while women are given the area of praise. When God is moving at this point, He moves with His entire throne. All this time it was just the men worshipping Yahweh. Then David puts down his harp, and he hands over the stage to Miriam the sister of Moses, and then she begins to lead the choir composed of the mighty women of God. They sing praises unto the Lord. Women are better at praises than men. As Miriam begins to sing praises unto the Most High, all of Heaven begins to dance including the angels. Even the seraphim who guard the gates of Heaven dance a little bit while staying on guard. Nobody gets tired as they are dancing because the joy of the Lord is their strength. As the Lord is pleased with His creation as they dance and sing unto Him, He is pleased and as His joy increases and as the joy of the King increases, the strength and energy of His people also increases.

> *"Then he said unto them, Go your way, eat the fat, and drink the sweet, and send portions unto them for whom nothing is prepared: for this day is holy unto our Lord: neither be ye sorry; for the joy of the Lord is your strength." (Nehemiah 8:10)*

Dancing And Singing

Nobody who is dancing in that place sweats and nobody gets thirsty, neither do they tire. People in Heaven eat because they want to eat, not because they are hungry. This is why it is written in Deuteronomy 8:3:

> "And he humbled thee, and suffered thee to hunger, and fed thee with manna, which thou knewest not, neither did thy fathers know; that he might make thee know that man doth not live by bread only, but by every word that proceedeth out of the mouth of the Lord doth man live."

As they dance and praise, they look younger and younger. Even ten times younger. In Heaven there is no aging. The only thing that may reveal someone's age is their white hair which comes out as glory. In Heaven, age is glory.

> "The hoary head is a crown of glory, if it be found in the way of righteousness." (Proverbs 16:31)

Hoary means gray, or white in color. You see the one who is praising must praise in all dimensions, and the one who is worshipping must worship in all dimensions. They sing worship songs which are known in the earth and in Heaven and beyond the Heavens. Once they have praised and worshipped in all dimensions until the King is well pleased, they step aside. Then the angels begin to display all of their skills before the throne of God. The way the angels display their skills in Heaven is similar to the way the Air Force will display some of their prized supersonic jets which break the sound barrier and climb suddenly to dizzying heights. They display their skills to honor the Great King who lives forever and ever. After the angels have displayed their skills, Enoch begins to roll from one side of the throne to the other as all of

Heaven goes down prostrate upon their faces. Enoch does this twelve times, and then the kings and the elders surrender their crowns and prostrate themselves before the Lord.

CHAPTER FOURTEEN - GOD

Then Almighty God rises in His Might and He begins to walk towards His creation. Every step He makes is calculated because His steps have consequences in all of the dimensions of existence. He moves with such immaculate and calculated grace down the steps. His splendor and majesty are too resplendent to describe. Even the greatest poets, the most brilliant orators, the masters of english literature and all of the ancient writers of old combined, can not do Him justice!

Oh Father!

When He stands up, all of creation sees a Father. I cannot estimate His height or size because He cannot be measured or weighed. If He wants to, His feet can step on the surface of the earth while His height stretches to the Highest of the Heavens. The color of His skin is fire. He is not black or white or yellow or brown, He is a consuming fire! His hair is like fine white sheep's wool and so are His eyebrows and His beard is pure white. There is nothing in this world that can be compared to the whiteness of His hair, eye brows, mustache and beard. The pupil of His eye is orange fire and this fire can even come out of His eyes. His nose is like the nose of a man but His nose does not inhale air. Instead it produces air continuously to all of His creation. Everything created is surviving on the supply of His air and His life force. Even the powers of darkness rely on His air to breath. When the scriptures say that in

Him we live and move and have our being, they do not lie:!

> *"For in him we live, and move, and have our being; as
> certain also of your own poets have said, ``For we are also
> his offspring." (Acts 17:28)*

His mouth is shaped like ours (really our mouths are shaped like His) but with perfectly fine, well shaped teeth. His smile is the smile of a Father. His tongue is pure fire similar to the shapes of our tongues but His is flames and when He speaks His words come out in the form of smoke. He speaks calmly with authority. His words light up the Heavens like lightening and go beyond the Heavens and the earth, like thunder. He does not just speak, because He is His Word and His word is Him. Anything that He speaks will complete its purpose with the same power and integrity that He possesses as God.

He wears a robe that matches with His color, it is orange in color and He matches it with a golden belt that is perfectly fastened around His waist and His feet are adorned with golden sandals. I'm talking about pure gold, the likes of which does not exist in this physical dimension called the earth. His hands are far larger than a normal person's hands. The palms of His hands are not smooth like ours. They are full of His works, they are rough, full of marks, including the marks where the nails went through His wrists, but they are the most beautiful hands I've ever seen. His feet are not smooth like ours. His feet are ancient, but perfect and beautiful to look upon. His nails are ancient - He is the Ancient of Days, like one who has passed through every kind of test and purification process and has been through more than we can imagine. When we ordinary human beings stand up, our shadow is black. His shadow is not black like ours. Our shadows are black because of our sinful and fallen nature. His shadow is pure light. So when David the psalmist speaks in Psalms 91:1 saying, *"He that dwells in* the secret place of the Most High, shall abide under the shadow of the almighty..." he is talking about the shadow of the Lord which is full of light. If we dwell under His shadow, the darkness has to flee. Dwelling under His shadow means abiding in His everlasting light which is His Word and abiding in His presence continuously.

> "After this manner therefore pray ye: Our Father which art in heaven, Hallowed be Thy Name." (Matthew 6:9)

> "Thy word is a lamp unto my feet, and a light unto my path." (Psalms 119:105)

In John 15:7 Jesus says,

> "If ye abide in me, and my words abide in you, ye shall ask what ye will, and it shall be done unto you."

> "The LORD reigneth; let the people tremble: he sitteth between the Cherubims; let the earth be moved." (Psalms 99:1)

Every time He smiles, all of His creation is renewed. Every time He is grieved, all of His creation is drained.

> "Kiss the Son, lest he be angry, and ye perish from the way, when his wrath is kindled but a little. Blessed are all they that put their trust in him." (Psalms 2:12)

When He laughs, all of His enemies are judged. During spiritual warfare, do something that brings laughter to the Lord. Your enemies will be scattered. Even the memory of them will perish from the earth.

*"He that sitteth in the heavens shall laugh: the Lord shall
have them in derision. Then shall He speak unto them in
His wrath, and vex them in His sore displeasure." Psalms
2:4,5)*

You never want God to laugh at you. It's better that He smiles at
you, His laughter as a result of your evil plans will blot out your
existence.

*"The memory of the just is blessed: but the name of the
wicked shall rot." (Proverbs 10:7)*

Those who despise the Lord will perish from the earth.

*"Whoso despiseth the word shall be destroyed: but he that
feareth the commandment shall be rewarded." (Proverbs
13:13)*

The features of God which I have described here are the features
which resemble a man because God has four faces and what I have
described above only scratches the surface of the face which re-
sembles that of a man.

CHAPTER FIFTEEN – MY CONVERSATION WITH GOD

The same angel that had helped me before opened the gate and as soon as I entered the gate I saw a very old but strong and healthy man. His hair was natural like wool but pure white. The color of his skin was like the color of orange flames of fire. This man was wearing an orange robe but in His waist was a golden belt fastened very neatly. He was wearing shoes that were pure gold. The angel told me that He is the Ancient of Days. He said that He sits upon His holy hill and watches over everything that He has created. The angel said that He likes positioning Himself between the physical and spiritual worlds. By the time the angel was describing Him, I was looking at His back. The angel also mentioned to me that He is the Father of the universe. He told me that the earth and its fullness belongs to Him. He said, "it was from Him that we became." As soon as the angel said that, I just wanted to go over and touch my Father. As I was walking over to touch Him, He said "don't touch me child, it's not yet time." Then I saw Him ascend into a hill and He sat on a rock. Where He was standing, He left marks of His footprints. They were the footprints of a very ancient foot. I tried to put my own feet where He had stepped but my foot was like a little doll's foot compared to His foot size. When I saw how much bigger His foot was I said "Woooooooow!" Then He laughed gently. His laugh was genuine. He laughed from within. His laugh is the laugh of the Father, full of love, peace and life. If you hear Him laugh you will also laugh!

My Questions To The Almighty

I had requested the Cherub Fierce to talk to God. I had seen those dimensions of God. By the time He stood up from His throne, I was already down on the ground and my face was on the floor. Even when my face was on the floor and my eyes were closed, I could still see Him clearly. There was nowhere to hide. The only words I remember coming out of my mouth were, "Oh mighty one have mercy on me! I have rebelled against you and I have worked against you for a long time because I was initiated into the kingdom of darkness by my grandmother without my consent. But through my mother and your servants, you sent Michael to rescue my soul and bring it back into my body. I have heard so many good things about you, but I had never come to your Kingdom before. I served you because I was told that it was the only way to be safeguarded from the attacks of Satan. Even then, I served faithfully. By the time I died, I was coming from a one week conference and I died on my way back home. Even before I died, I called upon the name of the Lord, but the more I called, the more pain I had and the more blood flushed out of my legs. I did not know that you are this wealthy, because we, your servants, are wallowing in poverty. Sometimes I didn't even have enough money for food. I died with only six pairs of torn and worn out shoes. When I came here, even your servants were wearing gold and silver shoes. My family struggles to put food on the table and yet they serve you and here there is all kinds of food that is not even being consumed. From my childhood I have only known pain, betrayal and witchcraft, in fact, I died in pain. Yet here, your joy is everyone's strength. I know I have not been the best person on earth but with what I've been through, I beg to stay here where there is no worry, no pain, no witchcraft, no sorrow, no misery, no jealousy and no fear." Then I told Him, "Surely, in your presence is fullness of joy." The moment I told Him that, He smiled and started to walk towards me. His first step down was from the seventh to the sixth Heaven. Then from the sixth Heaven to the fifth Heaven and I began to shout "Stooooooop, don't come!" I was feeling consumed by His presence! I was not even prepared for it. When I requested that He should not move forward from the place where He was, He stopped. If I would've known then, what I know now, I would have just allowed Him to come despite how overwhelming His actual presence is.

He Speaks!

Then that is when I heard Him speak. He said, "My friend." I was shocked that He called me "His friend." Because I knew for a long time that I had been His enemy for eighteen years, and now He was calling me His friend. He continued, "If you were to stay here, where would you be?" I replied, "in the second Heaven." I knew because He had only come down two steps and I was being overwhelmed. So the second Heaven is where I would have been comfortable.

Then He asked me, "And where would you like to be if you died?" And I replied, "at least in the sixth or the seventh Heaven because the closer to you the better." Then He said, "When you were born, the world issued you a birth certificate, I issued you a birth certificate before you entered into your mother's womb. Today, they are about to issue you a death certificate which I have not issued you, meaning, you only have a short time here. I allowed you to come here because I wanted to reveal myself to you. I want to reveal myself to my children. But their hearts are so far from me. Their hearts are tied to material things that will come to an end. In fact, nothing in the world satisfies. The only satisfaction you will get is when you abide in Me and I in you. I called you to serve me, therefore I demand that you don't look at the pastors that you're working with. Look at me all the time. If you look at man, you will stumble and fall."

Then He said, "Not everyone who says unto me, Lord Lord, will enter into my Kingdom. Don't judge men and women by miracles, signs and wonders. Judge them by My fruit. Patience, peace, long suffering, kindness, meekness, gentleness, faith and generosity. Most of My servants are not really known by men. But I and the Heavens recognize them. Most of the miracles you see on TV are not from Me. They are cooked up stories, and some are from Pharaoh." Then He told me, "The people who do real miracles do not even want to be spoken about." Then He said, "If you serve Me faithfully, I will honor you, and confirm your words with miracles, signs and wonders; but, remember not to take My place. I am God, I will always remain God."

Then I asked Him about why some people are very rich and popular and they are in the kingdom of darkness, while the servants of the Lord are very poor. He answered, "do not panic when you see the wicked flourishing, do not envy their wealth, because they labor in vain, and my children will inherit their wealth." Then I said, "But all the same, I don't want to go back, please I beg you." Then He smiles and said, "You cannot be my friend and be in the second Heaven, go and serve me and I will send my angels to work with you. I will send you help from all over the world. And after you have fulfilled your purpose, I will surely reward you."

His Holy Hill

After I saw God ascending and descending from His Holy hill, I also requested that I be able to ascend and descend as well. He allowed me to fly and watched me as I ascended and descended. I was screaming with joy. After this He told me that He would be manifesting Himself to me and revealing to me what He desires for me to do. Then Fierce escorted me back to my body. I opened my eyes when the doctor was asking my mother if I had regained consciousness yet. When my mother looked at me she said, "She has just now opened her eyes." The doctors checked for every disease possible. Every test came back negative. My three death experiences

were as a result of witchcraft but God decided to show Himself strong on my behalf.I will forever give glory to His name for His mercy and faithfulness and His grace towards the children of men.

CHAPTER SIXTEEN - LEAVING HEAVEN

Then, the moment He spoke those words, I could see what was happening back on the earth. I could see all of the nations of the world. I also saw that the world is full of noise and so much activity. So much so, that even when God speaks, nobody hears Him. I saw one of my relatives call my mother and tell my mother that my situation is bad and they're waiting to hear anything from the doctor. Meanwhile the doctor was telling the nurse that I was dead and that she should dress my body and take me to the mortuary. So now my mother began to speak and say, "Let God remind me of the covenant that I made with Him concerning my daughter serving Him, because I have been the one reminding Him, and now it is His turn to remind me."

God Answers My Mother's Prayer

Then God spoke immediately and said, "Erica, go back and serve Me, go back to your mother. Then, as soon as He spoke those words, I was consumed by a light that brought me back to the cold tunnel where the whirlwind sucked me back into the world and I found myself on top of the roof of the hospital, then I went right through the roof and into the ward and I entered into the room at the exact same time as the nurse who was coming to dress my dead body and prepare it for the mortuary. I entered my body through my head and it was like I was putting on a pair of pants, one pant leg at a time. Once I fit properly into my body, a light struck me like a jumpstart battery and it activated my bodily systems. It was my spirit that had been restored to my body and my heart began to pump again. Then I opened my eyes while the nurse was preparing a huge injection syringe filled with chemicals used to preserve dead bodies from rotting. When she saw my eyes opening, she threw the bedsheets and took off running to call the doctor. The doctor came into the room where I was.

I was now beginning to regain my senses. I had woken up to the world of pain. Everything in this world is vanity. In my next book, I will discuss my different encounters with angels with my husband. But one thing I want you all to know is that everything that took place in Heaven, from my death to my return into my body took approximately thirty minutes. This is because the spiritual world is not limited by time. In the spiritual world, you can travel ahead of time, and you can travel back in time or you can travel into time itself. Moses traveled back in time and was able to narrate what He saw in the beginning.

Your Heavenly Investment

With my experience, I would advise the reader to invest more into their spiritual well-being than their physical well-being. Invest in your eternal future, because when you die, everything you worked for will fade away, and the only thing that matters is the investment you made in eternity.

> "Heaven and earth shall pass away, but my words shall not pass away." (Matthew 24:35)

If you have not surrendered your life to the Lord Jesus Christ. I would love for you to say the following prayer. The evil which will be deployed upon the face of the earth in the very near future will include, plagues, pestilences, the opening of portals which will allow the armies of Hell to invade the earth. Beings, creatures, monsters, worse than anything you ever imagined will torment the inhabitants of the earth. They will kill, steal and destroy, because that is what Satan comes to do. Prepare yourself for the coming days and for eternity itself.

Pray this prayer with me.

"Heavenly Father I come to you because you have drawn me to yourself by your goodness. I have heard your Word. I believe that Jesus is Lord and I confess with my mouth that God raised Jesus from the dead. Forgive me of my sins. Holy Spirit please make your abode in me. Find expression through this life. In Jesus name I pray."

> "God standeth in the congregation of the mighty; he judgeth among the gods. How long will ye judge unjustly, and accept the persons of the wicked? Selah. Defend the poor and fatherless: do justice to the afflicted and needy. Deliver the poor and needy: rid them out of the hand of the wicked. They know not, neither will they understand; they walk on in darkness: all the foundations of the earth are out of course. I have said, Ye are gods; and all of you are children of the most High. But ye shall die like men, and fall like one of the princes.
> Arise, O God, judge the earth: for thou shalt inherit all nations." (Psalms 82:1-8)

The body of Christ is called, through Christ Jesus, unto the rank and stature of God-hood to be sons of God. Meaning, we are to so grow in Christ and Christ is to so grow in us that our lives become proof that Jesus rose from the dead. An atheist should be forced to look at our lives and question his atheism.

Blessed Koinonia

When the attention of man is pointed towards the cross of Jesus Christ and people hear that their debt for sins committed either by them or their ancestors has been paid, the demons, curses, spells, afflictions, witchcraft, oppressing them are forced to relinquish their hold on humanity because there is no legal right for them to stay.

This blessed reunion is what God had in mind from the beginning when Adam sinned and mankind fell from glory in a moment. Mankind belongs to the God-class. Out of all of God's creation, man is the only creation which can carry the presence of God inside of him. I will elaborate about this later. No other creature in all of creation enjoys this union. This is koinonia. The blessed union of divinity with humanity. God gave everything so that this union could be possible, even Himself!

> *"Be patient therefore, brethren, unto the coming of the Lord. Behold, the husbandman waiteth for the precious fruit of the earth, and hath long patience for it, until he receives the early and latter rain." (James 5:7)*

Amen!

Made in the USA
Coppell, TX
13 November 2024

40142621R00063